Management Policies and Practices of Micro, Small and Medium Scale Industries in India

Dr.S. Thangaraju

Published by

Management Policies and Practices of Micro, Small and Medium Scale Industries in India

ISBN 978-93-86176-05-9

Author

Dr.S. Thangaraju

Bonfring
309, 2nd Floor, 5th Street Extension, Gandhipuram,
Coimbatore-641 012.
Tamilnadu, India.
E-mail: info@bonfring.org | Website: www.bonfring.org
Phone: 0422-3928700

Preface

India is a country comprised of millions of Micro, Small and medium scale entrepreneurs. The Government may not provide the Employment for all people. Hence, it encourages the MSMEs to get started and Established by providing many support. Therefore, they framed the policies and procedures that guide MSMEs in the country. This book gives a good coverage on all the nuance of MSMEs sector. This book is useful and vital for MSMEs Enterprises and their employees to define their management strategies and other proceeded to uplift their business activities. Besides, this book will also help the students to learn about MSMEs in Indian. What are the changes have been made and paradigm shift is emerged in this sector? The recent policies and schemes where pertaining to MSMEs have adapted in accordance with industrial sector and competing for global competency. This information is elaborately explained with evidences from recent Annual report and parliament proceedings.

| Chapter | **Contents** | **Page No** |

CHAPTER-I

NATURE AND SCOPE OF SMALL SCALE INDUSTRIES POLICIES AND PRACTICES

1.1. Introduction

Micro, Small and Medium Enterprises (MSME) sector has emerged as a highly vibrant and dynamic sector of the Indian economy over the last five decades. MSMEs not only play crucial role in providing large employment opportunities at comparatively lower capital cost than large industries but also help in industrialization of rural & backward areas, thereby, reducing regional imbalances, assuring more equitable distribution of national income and wealth. MSMEs are complementary to large industries as ancillary units and this sector contributes enormously to the socioeconomic development of the country. Khadi is the proud legacy of our national freedom movement and the father of the nation. Khadi and Village Industries (KVI) are two national heritages of India. One of the most significant aspects of KVI in Indian economy is that it creates employment at a very low per capita investment. The KVI Sector not only serves the basic needs of processed goods of the vast rural sector of the country but also provides sustainable employment to rural artisans. KVI today represent an exquisite, heritage product, which is 'ethnic' as well as 'ethical'. The Sector has a potentially strong clientele among the middle and upper echelons of the society. (*Government of India: 2013-14, p3*)

1.2. Small Scale and Cottage Industries–Definition and Meaning

1.2.1. *Small Scale Industries*

An industrial undertaking in which the investment in fixed assets in plant & machinery, whether held on ownership terms, or on lease, or by hire purchase, does not exceed `100 lakh as on 31-03-2001 were be treated as a Small Scale Industrial Unit.

1.2.2. *Micro Small Medium Enterprises (MSME)*

Micro, small and medium enterprises as per MSMED Act, 2006 are defined based on their investment in plant and machinery (for manufacturing enterprise) and on equipment for enterprises providing or rendering services.

The present ceilings on investment for enterprises to be classified as micro, small and medium enterprises are as follows:

Table 1.1: Classification of Small Industries

Classification	Manufacturing Enterprises*	Service Enterprises**
Micro	Rs. 2.5 million / Rs. 25 lakh (US$ 50,000)	Rs. 1 million / Rs. 10 lakh (US$ 20000)
Small	Rs.50 million / Rs. 5 crore (US$ 1 million)	Rs. 20 million / Rs 2 crore (US$ 0.4 million)
Medium	Rs 100 million / Rs 10 crore (US$ 2 million)	Rs. 50 million / Rs 5 crore (US$ 1 million)

Source: MSME Annual Report -2014-15, Government of India pp-296

*Investment limit in Plant & Machinery ***

*Investment limit in equipment*** Rs 50 = 1 US$*

MSME Sector consists of any enterprises, whether proprietorship, Hindu undivided family, association of persons, co-operative society, partnership or undertaking or any other legal entity, by whatever name called, engaged in production of goods pertaining to any industry specified in the first schedule of Industry Development & Regulation Act, 1951 and other enterprises engaged in production and rendering services, subject to limiting factor of investment in plant and machinery and equipments:

Table 1.2: Evolution of Investment Limits for Small Scale Industries

S.No	Year	Investment limits	Additional conditions
1	1950	Up to Rs. 0.5 Million in Fixed Assets	Less than 50/100 persons with or without power
2	1960	Up to Rs. 0.5 Million in Fixed Assets	No condition
3	1966	Up to Rs. 0.5 Million in Fixed Assets	No condition
4	1975	Up to Rs. 1 Million in Plant and Machinery	No condition
5	1980	Up to Rs. 2 Million in Plant and Machinery	No condition
6	1985	Up to Rs. 3.5 Million in Plant and Machinery	No condition
7	1991	Up to Rs. 6 Million in Plant and Machinery	No condition
8	1997	Up to Rs. 30 Million in Plant and Machinery	No condition
9	1999 to onward	Up to Rs. 10 Million in Plant and Machinery	No condition

Source: Udyog Yug -July 2004

The above table illustrated the investment limits   fixed and revised by the Government of India from time to time for the development and Sanction of the subsidiaries to SSI sector in India.

1.2.3. *Village Industries*

The term *"village industries"* has been redefined in amended KVIC, Act, 1956 as "any industry located in a rural area which produces any goods or renders any service with or without the use of power and in which the fixed capital investment per head of artisan or worker does not exceed Rs. one lakh (Rs. one lakh and fifty thousand in case of village industry located in a hilly area) or such other sum as may, by notification in the Official Gazette, be specified from time to time by the Central Government

The Government has also enhanced the investment ceiling in respect of group of products falling under the category Hand Tools and Hosiery to Rs. 5 cores, similar enhancements may be accorded to several other high tech export thrust items.

1.2.4. *Tiny Sector*

The Tiny sector has also been identified, At present this includes s having investment in fixed assets in plant and machinery not exceeding Rs.5lakhs and situated in rural and backward areas having population up to 50,000 as per 1981 census.

Small scale service establishments/enterprises are those engaged in personal or household services in rural areas and towns with population of 5lakhs or less and having investment in plant and machinery not exceeding Rs.2lakhs.

1.2.5. *Cottage Industry*

According to definition of the Fiscal commission in 1950 " A Cottage industry is one which is carried on wholly or primarily with the help of the members of the family. Either as a whole or a part –time occupation, a small scale industry, on the other hand, is one which is operated mainly with hired labour, usually 10 to 15 hands

According to this definition, the industries Development and Regulation (IDRA) Act, 1951 gave exemption to units employing less than 50 workers without power, from registration. This exempted sector has come to be known as the "Small-Scale Sector"

1.2.6. Ancillary Units

Undertakings having investment in the fixed assets in plant and machinery not exceeding Rs.75 lakhs with the following features are called ancillary units.

a) The investment in fixed assets in plant and machinery, whether held on ownership terms or by lease or by hire-purchase, does not exceed Rs.75lakhs; and

b) The undertaking is engaged or proposed to be engaged in the manufacture or production of parts, components, sub-assemblies, tooling or intermediates, or the rendering of services, and the undertaking supplies or renders or proposes to supply or render at least 30% of its production or service, as the case may be to one or more other industrial undertakings. Provided that, no small scale or ancillary industrial undertakings referred to above shall be subsidiary of, or owned or controlled by, any other industrial undertaking.

1.3.   Characteristics of Small Scale Industries

According to the Committee of Economics development (USA) a small business is one which possesses at least two of the following four characteristics.

1. Management of the firm is independent. Usually the managers are also the owners.
2. Capital is supplied and the ownership is held by an individual or a small group.
3. The area of operation is mainly local, with the workers and owners living in one home community. However, the markets need not be local.
4. The relative size of the firm within its industry must be small when compared with the biggest units in its field. These measures can be of sales volume, number of employees or other significant comparisons.

The basis of distinctions between the large scale, medium scale and small scale industries is generally the size, capital resource and workers force of the one each one unit.

1.4.   Vision, Mission and Objectives of Small Scale Industries in India

The Functions Results-Framework Document (RFD) for Ministry of Micro, Small and Medium Enterprises-(2013-2014) describes the vision, mission and objectives of small scale sector as follows

1.4.1. Vision

Sustainable development of globally competitive Micro, Small and Medium Enterprises as an engine of growth for the Indian Economy.

1.4.2. Mission

Mission Promote growth and development of Micro, Small and Medium Enterprises, including Khadi, Village and Coir industries, so as to achieve a cumulative growth of 50% in the number of registered enterprises and to enhance contribution to GDP to 10% by 2016-17.

1.4.3. Objectives

- Growth and development of existing MSMEs
- Creation of new enterprises
- Enhancing manufacturing base
- Skill and entrepreneurship development for MSMEs
- Growth and development of Khadi, Village and Coir industries
- Improving performance of PSU and Responsibility Centres

1.4.4. Functions Facilitation of Credit Flow to MSMEs

1. Improving competitiveness of MSMEs
2. Improve manufacturing base through up gradation of technology
3. Promotion of MSMEs through cluster based approach
4. Marketing support to MSMEs
5. Skill development and entrepreneurship development training
6. Creation of new Micro Enterprises through Prime Minister's Employment Generation Program (PMEGP)
7. Growth and development of Khadi and Village Industries (KVI) sector
8. Growth and development of Coir Industry

1.5. Categorization of Small Scale Industries

The Small scale industries may classified on the base of Production, Investment and Registration as discussed below

1.5.1. Production Based Classification

They have been categorized broadly into those engaged in

(i) Manufacturing and

(ii) Providing/ rendering of services.

i.   **Manufacturing Enterprises**: An industrial undertaking carrying the Manufacturing process in which the investment in fixed assets in plant and machinery, whether held on ownership terms, or on lease, or by hire purchase, does not exceed Rs. 10 crores as on 31-3-2007 is to be treated as manufacturing enterprises.

ii.   **Service Enterprises**: An enterprise engaged in providing/ rendering of services, in which the investment in Equipment, whether held on ownership terms, or on lease, or by hire purchase, does not exceed Rs. 5 crores as on 31-3-2007 is to be treated as a services enterprises.

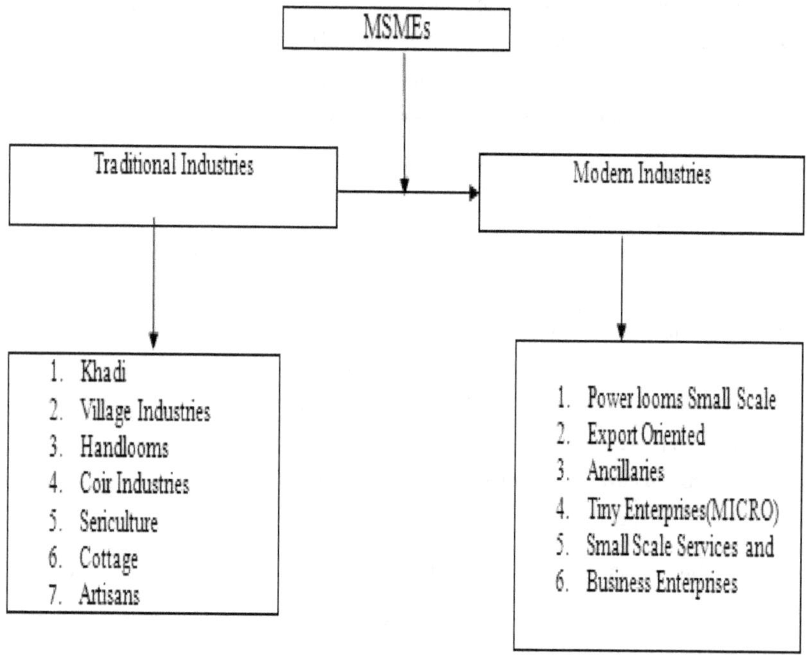

Chart 2.1: Manufacturing Based Classification of MSMEs

1.5.2. Investment Based Classification

Both above said categories have been further classified into micro, small and medium enterprises, based on their investment in plant and machinery (for manufacturing enterprises) or in equipment (in case of enterprises providing/rendering services) as under:

Table 1.3: Investment Based Classification of SSIs Units

S.No	Classification	Manufacturing enterprises	Service enterprises
1	Micro Enterprises	Fixed Investment in Plant & Machinery up to Rs. 25 lakh	Fixed Investment in Equipment up to Rs. 10 lakh
2	Small Enterprises	Fixed Investment in Plant & Machinery above Rs. 25 lakh & up to Rs. 5 crore.	Fixed Investment in Equipment above Rs. 10 lakh & up to Rs. 2 crore
3	Medium Enterprises.	Fixed Investment in Plant & Machinery above Rs. 5 crore& up to Rs. 10 crore	Fixed Investment in Equipment above Rs. 2 crore & up to Rs. 5 crore

Source: Compiled from MSME Act -2006

1.5.3. Registration Based Classification

1. **Registered Enterprises**: All enterprises engaged in the activities of manufacturing or in providing/rendering of services, registered permanently or filed Entrepreneurs Memorandum (EM) with State Directorates of Industries/District Industries Centres as on 31-3-2007 are called registered enterprises.

   Enterprises registered with District Industries Centres in the State/UTs., Khadi and Village Industries Commission/Khadi and Village Industries Board, Coir Board as on 31.03.2007 and factories under the coverage of section 2m (i) and 2m (ii) of the Factories Act 1948 used for Annual Survey of Industries having investment in plant & machinery up to Rs.10 crore were considered to belong to registered sector

2. **Unregistered Enterprises**: All enterprises engaged in the activities of manufacturing or in providing/rendering of services, not registered permanently or not filed EM with State Directorates of Industries/District Industries Centres on or before 31-3-2007 are called unregistered enterprises. Those enterprises that are temporarily registered on or before 31-3-2007 as also the units that are temporarily or permanently registered or filed EM after 31-32007 till the date of survey will be treated as unregistered enterprises for the purpose of this survey.

Table 1.4: The Economic Activities of Services and Manufacturing Enterprises

Name of Economic Activities	Whether relevant for MSME Sector
Agriculture, Hunting & Forestry, Fishing, Mining and Quarrying	None of these activities are relevant for MSME Sector. However services activities incidental to these may be 263 considered.
Manufacturing: Division 15 to 37 of NIC 2004	All activities are relevant for MSME Sector.
Electricity, Gas and Water Supply	All activities are relevant for MSME, except for Generation and Transmission of Electricity through Hydro-electric, coal based thermal, oil based thermal and atomic reactor power plants. Construction
Construction	These include Plumbing and Drainage, Installation of Heating & air conditioning system, antennas, elevators and escalators, insulation work, sound proofing system, Electric installation work, Setting of wall and Floor tiles, Building finishing work, Finish Carpentry, Water Fittings and Renting of construction of demolition equipment with operator
Maintenance and Repair of Motor Vehicles and Motorcycles	All activities are relevant for MSME Sector.
Repairs of personal and household goods	All activities are relevant for MSME Sector
Wholesale and Retail Trade	Though all the activities are relevant for MSME Sector,
Hotels and Restaurants	Though all the activities are relevant for MSME Sector,
Supporting & Auxiliary transport activities; Activities of Travel agencies	The activities like Cargo Handling, Storage & Warehousing, Activities of travel agencies and Tour operators and other transport agencies
Post and Telecommunications	These include Courier activities other than National post activities, Telecommunications.
Real Estate Activities	These include Real estate activities on a fee or contract basis.
Renting of Machinery and Equipment without operator and of Personal & Household goods	All activities are relevant for MSME Sector.
Computer and Related Activities	All activities are relevant for MSME Sector.
Other Business Activities	These includes Legal, Accounting, Book-keeping & Auditing activities; Tax consultancy Market research and public opinion polling; Business management and consultancy; Advertising, Packaging and other activities
Education	These include Coaching Centres and Activities relating to training / education / conduct of specialized course in computer knowledge
Health and Social work	All the activities are relevant for MSMEs, except for Govt. Hospitals and Private Nursing Homes
Other Service Activities	These include Washing and Cleaningof Textile & Fur products, Hair dressing / Cutting & other beauty treatment and other service activities e.g. marriage bureaus, shoe shiners, porters, valet car parkers, massage salons, sauna and steam baths, pet boarding, etc.

Source: The Final Report of the fourth all Indian census of small, micro enterprises 2006-2007.

1.6. Significance of Small Scale Industries

- The many characteristics of small Industries improve their deep-seated position in accelerating economic growth in the countries where they are seriously being developed.

- Their flexibility makes them best suited in environment where intervening variables play a large part in day-today business management.

- The small scale organization have a better change to carry out a number of innovations like combinations of new products, new materials, new methods of production, new markets, new sources of materials and even new forms of organization.

- Being change-susceptible and highly reactive to socio economic influences on the outside, small enterprise can easily adapt to and adopt measures that will ensure not only their own viability but also the growth of the economy in which they are situated.

- Being fairly labour intensive, they provide an economic solution by creating employment and income opportunities in urban and rural areas as a labour intensive industry with low capital investment.

- Decentralization and dispersal of industries into rural areas prevent the internal migration of unemployed rural youth to nearby urban area.

- SSIs is an important machinery to more balanced growth of economy in the whole country.

- By using indigenous raw materials and the promotion of intermediate and capital goods, small, enterprises can contribute to faster economic growth in a transitional economy.

- Being set up individuals, they provide a productive outlet of expressing the entrepreneurial spirit of human resources

1.7. Advantages of Small Scale Industries

The benefits of small scale industries can therefore, be summarized as follows:

1. Utilising local resources.
2. Creating jobs at relatively low capital cost (lower capital/labour ratio).
3. Diversifying industrial structure and following monopolies.
4. Providing a vehicle for introducing a more equitable income distribution.
5. Attracting and utilizing indigenous entrepreneurship.

6. Developing a pool of skilled and semi-skilled workers as a basis for future industrial expansion.

7. Improving forward and backward linkages between economically, socially and geographically diverse sectors of the economy.

8. Providing opportunities for developing and adapting appropriate technological and managerial approaches.

9. Increasing mobility for the improved development of natural resources.

10. Adapting flexibility to market changes.

1.8. The Contribution of SSI Sector towards the Economic Development

The small scale and cottage industries of India have a decisive role to play in the economic development of the country. By and large, small enterprises have certain definite advantages, which contribute to the economic well being of the nation.

1. Contribution to National Income

The small scale enterprises of India were contributing a large share of national when India became Independent. Only with the industrialization of the country, the share of large industries has gone up. Although there has been considerable development of large scale industries during the period of planning even now India remains mainly of small–scale production.

2. Employment Potential

The small scale industries are Labour Intensive–Labour investment ratio in their case in quite high. A given amount of capital invested in small scale industrial undertaking is likely to provide more employment, than the same amount of capital invested in large scale industries. This is a very important factor for a country like India where millions of people are unemployed and under-employed. Hence, it is a solution to the unemployment problem. As estimated by planning commission on the basis of 43rd round of National sample Survey (NSS), the open unemployment in April 1992 was estimated to be 17 million and the unemployment rates rise with every successive level of education. The additional employment generation on an average per year was 6.5 million.

The organized sector accounted for hardly 0.3 million. Therefore, most of the employment generation both in the public and organized private sectors are on the decrease, and, it is expected that much demand may not be forthcoming from such sectors. Unemployed youth, therefore, will have to concentrate on unorganised sectors, try to go in for small scale industries and carryout self-employment activities.

3. *Capital Light*

Small industries require only a smaller amount of capital than required by large scale industries. Where there is Scarcity of capital and economising capital is essential, small scale is the only effective solution. Moreover, small industries offer good scope for those who want to make really small beginning and then make a mark on the industrial map of the state and the country. Numerous are such industrial units, which can be started with an investment of 1 to 2 lakhs rupees, that too obtained from banks as loan.

4. *Skill Light*

In our country the supply of qualified personnel is very much limited and economizing the services of these people is also essential. Small scale industries do not require high degree of skill and managerial talent of engineers, technicians, accountants, etc. Small scale provides the training ground for industrial experience.

5. *Import Light*

Small scale industries do not depend too much on imported materials,(they mostly require indigenous machines & equipments), unlike large scale industries in which, heavy engineering equipment, machines and even raw materials have to be imported, which would create problems of foreign exchange earnings. Small industries reduce the need for foreign capital of foreign exchange earnings.

6. *Rapid acquiescent and Decentralization*

The time lag between investment and return in the case of small industries is very short and as such the project would give quick returns. Further, the small industries being distributed throughout the country, there will be no regional imbalance as in the case of large industries which are concentrated in some regions.

*7. **Better Distribution of Wealth**

The decentralisation of industries in the small scale sector secures even distribution of income and wealth. Large scale industries tend to concentrate large wealth in a few hands which is undesirable in a socialistic pattern of society. Further, small scale industry will not create slums, housing problems sanitation, disease and squalor as in the case of large industries.

1.9. Legal Frame work for SSIs Sector

The Micro, Small and Medium Enterprises Development (MSMED) Act, 2006 has been enacted to facilitate the promotion and development of micro, small and medium enterprises and enhancement of their competitiveness. The Act has come into effect from 2nd October, 2006.

The Micro, Small and Medium Enterprises Development (MSMED) Act confines the coverage and investment ceiling of the sector. The Act seeks to facilitate the development of these enterprises as also enhance their competitiveness. It provides the first-ever legal framework for recognition of the concept of "enterprise" which comprises both manufacturing and service entities. It defines medium enterprises for the first time and seeks to integrate the three tiers of these enterprises, namely, micro, small and medium. The Act also provides for a statutory consultative mechanism at the national level with balanced representation of all sections of stakeholders, particularly the three classes of enterprises and with a wide range of advisory functions. Establishment of specific funds for the promotion, development and enhancing competitiveness of these enterprises, notification of schemes/programmes for this purpose, progressive credit policies and practices, preference in Government procurements to products and services of the micro and small enterprises

CHAPTER-II

THE SMALL SCALE INDUSTRIES IN INDIA

2.1. Introduction

The Indian arts and crafts are known over from ancient times for intricate workmanship, exquisite nature and exclusive designs. India has the uniqueness of abundance of distinct varieties coming from various states within the state exclusive regions representing culture, usage, raw material base, craftsmanship, skills and techniques being practiced from generation to generation (*Government of India:2007-08, p-40*). This distinguished traditional craftsmanship and cultural arts pave the basement for the development of Indian small scale sector. The history of small-scale industry dates back to the Epic ages .The message of looms (Handloom Industry) are mentioned in the classical Indian text such as the Rig Veda and Atharvana Veda. The Message of the Ornament Factory and Ornament craftsmanship are mentioned in Silapathikaram (1 B.C to 3 B.C) of Tamil literature. Evidence of Madder-dyed fabric was found in Mohenjodaro and Harappa (*Ravikkumar.B: 2015,p-1)*

2.2. Historical Background of SSIs Sector

Since the Vedic age, Indian History exhibits the existence of craftsmanship based small scale industries. One of the significant reasons for the expansion of small scale sector in ancient days was that Indian civilization based on Caste System. The Indian society divided into four groups of castes such as Bhiramanas Sathiriyas, Vaysias and Suthiras. Duties and Responsibilities of each caste were well defined. The Bhiramans were the in charge of the Education and regions matter. The Sathiriyas were the in charge of government, public administration, Security and Justice. The Vaysias were the in-charge of the Commerce and Trade. This type of Vysiya community had the major responsibilities for establishment and development of small scale business. In this connection, birth decided once profession and the life style and day to day activities of particular family trained once profession. The person from weaving household became a very skilled weaver. The person from spot making community developed new production strategy, like wise all occupational based households developed their family based professional at small scale level.

This is basement or foundation for establishing and developing lakhs and lakhs of small scale industry in Indian sub continent. The second phase of small scale industrial development is due to industrial revolution of England and the spread of new technology based industries in British period (1850-1947). The third phase of current development in Small scale industries in India is due to present Institutional setup and industrial polices

2.2.1. Small Scale Sector in the Five Year Plans Period

The important aspect of the First five-year plan was the acceptance of the principle of a common production programme for large scale and small scale industries to eliminate competition between the two. This was formulated by

i)   Reserving of spheres of production.

ii) Limiting the expansion of large-scale industrial capacity.

iii) Arranging for the supply of raw materials.

iv) Co-coordinating research, training etc. and,

v)   Imposing chess on large scale industry.

For financing small scale and village industries, State Finance Corporation and National Small Industries Corporation were set up and rules governing grant of loans were liberalized. In order to encourage small and village industries, the government liberalized its store purchase policy by giving   preference to these products over the factory products up to a certain percentage. The planning commission appointed in June 1955. The village and Small Industries committee under the chairmanship of karve to examined the problems of small scale and cottage industries.

In the Second five year plan (1956-57 to 1960-61) the programme of village small industries was based on karve committee report. A provision of Rs.200 crores was made in this plan period for the development of handloom, khadi village and small industries including 'Ambar Charka' programme. Special stress was laid on the establishment of industrial co-operatives in every field. By 1960-61, 634 industrial estates were also constructed under the initiative of the government and a provision of Rs.15 crores was made available for this purpose in the second plan.

During this period, the government of India invited a 5 member Japanese delegation of exports headed by T. Iwatake to study the organization of small industries in India. The delegation recommended many change for the promotion of small industries.

During the Third Five year plan (1960-61 to 1965-66) the main objectives were to improve the productivity of the workers in small industries to enlarge the availability of institutional finance, promotion of small industries as ancillaries to large industries. During this plan period a sum of Rs.240.75 crores were spent on the development of cottage and small scale industries in India in the public sector.

The objectives of small industries programme in the Fourth five-year plan (1960-70 to 1973-74) were:

i) To improve the production techniques and enable them to produce quality goods and to bring them to a viable level

ii) To promote decentralization and dispersal of industries and

iii) To promote agro based industries.

These were expected to be achieved through giving facilities for

a) research

b) design and development

c) industrial extension services

d) enlarged testing and

e) promoting schemes for supply of machines on hire purchase with the assistance of the banks.

In the Fifth plan of 1974-75 to March 1978, the strategy of development was designed as follows;

a) Developing and promoting entrepreneurship and providing a 'package of consultancy service' so as to generate maximum employment and self employment opportunities;

b) Facilitating fuller utilization of the skills and equipment of the person, and, progressively improving the production techniques;

c) Promoting these industries in selected 'growth centers' in semi- urban and rural areas including backward areas.

For this purpose a total outlay of about Rs. 1,600 crores was made available for the development of small industries.

The Sixth five year plan (1980-85) envisaged further improvement in the levels of production, creation of additional employment opportunities, and expanded effort in export promotion.

The Seventh plan (1985-1990) allocated a sum fo Rs. 2,752.74 crores towards village and small scale industries. The small scale sector achieved the targets set in terms of production and employment this period. The value of exports from small scale sector went up from Rs.2553 crores in 1948-85 to RS.7626 crores in 1989-90. The number of small scale units under the purview of Small Industries Development Organisation (SIDO) (registered and un-registered) increased from 12 laths units at the end of 1948-85 to around 18lakhs units at the end of 1989-90.

The small scale industrial sector emerged as a dynamic and vibrant sector of the economy during the eighties. At the end of the seventh plan period, it accounted for nearly 55% of the gross value of output in the manufacturing sector and over 42% of the total exports from the country. It also provided employment opportunities to around 12.4 million people.

The Eighth five year plan (1992-97) is totally a different plan from earlier plans as it was formulated in a changed context of economic liberalization since 1991, which focuses among others oh Human development, employment in rural areas, setting up small 'Agri-Business consortium' to bring together farmers, the business community, banking institutions, scientific organisations and various governmental bodies. Ten areas have been identified. They are food crops, oilseeds, cotton, sugarcane, horticulture, sericulture, dairy development, poultry, aquaculture and agro-forestry for intensive attention. The objective is development, poultry, aquaculture and agro-forestry for intensive attention. The objective is to improve the efficiency of production and post-harvest technologies and develop suitable marketing network which would lead to creation of more jobs, as well as, income generation.

During 1993-94, the mall scale sector registered a growth rate of 7% as against 4% growth of large scale industries. In the export sector, the growth rate was 28% though the national average was just 20%. Small scale sector accounted for 40% of the total manufacturing outputs and 35% of the exports. The direct exports accounted for 33% and indirect exports 50% from this sector. There were about 24 laths registered small scale units in the country out of which nearly 8000 were ancillary units. The largest number of small scale industrial units had been found in Maharashtra, Gujarat, Uttarpradesh & Karnataka. It estimated that 80% of the units are distributed on 240 districts and about 140 laths were employed in small scale industries.

2.3.   Present Scenario of the MSME Sector in India

The micro, small and medium enterprises constitute a very important segment of the Indian economy. Today, it accounts for nearly 45% of the gross value of output in the Manufacturing Sector and over 40% of the total exports from the country.

In terms of value added, this sector accounts for about 40% of the value addition in the Manufacturing Sector. The sector's contribution to employment is second highest next to agriculture. It has been estimated that every one lakh rupees of investment in fixed assets in the MSMEs sector generates employment for about 0.21 persons as per IV All India Census of MSMEs.

The capability of Indian MSME products to compete in international markets is reflected in its share of about 40% in national exports. In case of items like readymade garments, leather goods, processed foods, engineering items, the performance has been commendable both in terms of value and their share within the MSME sector while in some cases like sports goods etc., they account for 100% share to the total exports of the sector. The MSME sector has consistently registered a higher growth rate compared with overall industrial sector. With its agility and dynamism, the sector has shown admirable innovativeness and adaptability to survive the economic downturn and recession (*Policy Note, Government of Tamil Nadu; 2014-1015 Pp- 5-6)*

2.3.1.   Distribution of Micro, Small and Medium Enterprise sector in India

The Fourth Census identified the distribution of Micro, Small and Medium enterprises throughout country.361.76 lakh of MSME are functioning very well in this country. Out of that, 115.01 lakh of manufacturing enterprises and 246.75 lakh service enterprises are estimated to providing its contribution to our National Income. At the beginning of SSIs Sector, Majority of the industries are the Manufacturing industries. But at present there is considerably change which indicates the domination of Services industries in this sector. This sector is providing the employment opportunities to 805.24 lakh peoples in our country. This is second largest sector in providing the employment opportunities to both skilled and semi skilled uneducated Indian workers. *(Table: 2.1)*

Table 2.1: Distribution of Micro, Small and Medium Enterprise Sector in India

(Figures in Lakhs)

S.No	Characteristics	Registered Sector	Unregistered Sector*	Total
1	Total number of working enterprises	15.64	346.12	361.76
	Manufacturing	10.5	104.51	115.01
	Services	5.14	241.61	246.75
2	Number of rural enterprises	7.07	193.12	200.19
3	Number of urban enterprises	8.57	153	161.57
4	Number of women enterprises	2.15	24.46	26.6
5	Number of enterprises running perennially	15.14	189.13	204.27
6	Employment	93.09	712.14	805.24
	Manufacturing	80.84	239.23	320.07
	Services	12.26	472.91	485.17
7	Employment	93.09	712.14	805.24
	Male	74.05	610.62	684.68
	Female	19.04	101.52	120.56
8	Enterprises by type of social category	15.64	346.12	361.76
	SC	1.19	27.15	28.34
	ST	0.45	20.4	20.84
	OBC	5.99	145.74	151.73
	Others	8.01	149.55	157.57
	Not Responded	0	3.27	3
9	Enterprises by type of organization	15.64	346.12	361.76
	Proprietary	14.09	327.45	341.54
	Partnership	0.63	3.65	4.28
	Private Company	0.43	0.06	0.49
	Co-operatives	0.05	1.16	1.21
	Others	0.44	7.65	8.09
	Not Recorded	0	6.15	6.15
10	Enterprises by main Source of power	15.64	346.12	361.76
	No Power needed	3.79	194.39	198.18
	Coal	0.25	6.23	6.48
	Oil	0.53	13.86	14.39
	LPG/CNG	0.07	3.97	4.04
	Electricity	10.49	106.52	117.01
	Non-Conventional Energy	0.03	0.85	0.88
	Traditional Energy/Firewood	0.23	7.15	7.39
	Others	0.25	10.19	10.44
	Not Recorde	0	2.95	2.95

Source: Msme Annual Report 2014-15, Government of India pp-234

*Note * - For activities excluded in Survey of fourth All India Census of MSME, Unregistered sector (Retail / Wholesale Trade Establishment, Legal Services, Educational Services, Social Services, Hotels & Restaurants, Transport, Storage & Warehousing (except Cold Storage) data were taken from Economic Census-2005, Central Statistics Office of Ministry of Statistics and Programme Implementation*

While on a strictly comparable basis, growth rate recorded during the year 2001-02 to 2006-07 was 15.30% and 15.02% for estimated number of Enterprises and Employment respectively, the sector as a whole recorded a growth rate of 28.02% and 26.42% in cases of estimated number of enterprises and employment respectively, taking into account the definitional changes during the period 2001-02 to 2006-07.

As the activities brought under the coverage of MSME sector due to definitional changes in 2006-07 were limited to services sector, the growth rate for manufacturing sector is comparable. The growth recorded during the year 2001-02 to 2006-07 in manufacturing sector was 22.46% and 18.49% for estimated number of enterprises and employment respectively.

For service sector, while the growth rate in estimated number of enterprises and employment recorded was 31.21% and 34.00% respectively, during the period of 2001-02 to 2006-07 taking into account the expanded coverage of the sector, the same was 9.39% and 10.12% respectively on strictly comparable basis Additional activities brought under the coverage of MSME Sector in 2006-07 as compared to SSI sector of 2001-02, namely wholesale/retail trade, legal, educational & social services, hotel & restaurants, transports and storage & warehousing (except cold storage), accounted for 12.72% and 11.40% growth in the estimated number of enterprises and employment respectively.

The estimated number of enterprises growth at 3.76% annually in case of manufacturing sector and 0.47% for services sector respectively in Registered Sector during 2001-02 to 2006-07, as per Fourth All India Census of MSME 2006-07, Registered Sector and Third All India Census of SSI 2001-02, Registered Sector. The growth in the estimated number of MSME was 2.61% for the period referred above, taking manufacturing and services together

The employment increased at an annual growth rate of 9.84% for manufacturing sector and 2.06% for services sector during 2001-02 to 2006-07, as per Fourth All India Census of MSME 2006-07, Registered Sector and Third All India Census of SSI 2001-02, Registered Sector. The employments in Registered Sector as a whole grow at 8.60% per annum during 2001-02 to 2006-07 as per Fourth All India Census of MSME 2006-07, Registered Sector and Third All India Census of SSI 2001-02, Registered Sector.

The estimated number of enterprises and employment recorded growth rates of 30.05% and 30.56%, respectively during the period 2001-02 to 2006-07 considering the extended coverage of the sector. The expansion in the coverage of MSME Sector followed adoption of Micro, Small and Medium Enterprises Act 2006. Activities pertaining to wholesale/retail trade, legal, educational & social services, hotel & restaurants, transports and storage & warehousing (except cold storage) which were brought under the coverage of MSME sector accounted for 147.38 and 303.31 lakh in terms of estimated number of enterprises and employment respectively, as per data extracted from Economic Census, 2005 conducted by Government of India for MSME relevant enterprises. The annual growth rates recorded, excluding these additional activities, were 16.79% and 16.85% in estimated number of enterprises and employment, respectively. The expansion in the coverage of MSME Sector was limited to service sector only. Therefore, the growth rate for manufacturing sector is not affected and the growth rate was recorded as 25.90% and 22.57% for estimated number of enterprises and employment respectively, during the year 2001-02 to 2006-07.

For service sector, while the growth rate of estimated number of enterprises and employment recorded was 32.83% and 36.11% respectively, during the period of 2001-02 to 2006-07, taking into account the expanded coverage of the sector, the growth rate was 10.03% and 10.88% in case of estimated number of enterprises and employment respectively on strictly comparable basis. Additional activities brought under the coverage of MSME Sector, namely wholesale/retail trade, legal, educational & social services, hotel & restaurants, transports and storage & warehousing (except cold storage), since the conduct of Third All India Census 2001-02 accounted for 13.71% points in the growth rate of number of enterprises and employment, respectively 2005

2.3.2. *State Wise Distribution of Small Scale Sector in India*

The ten leading States, in terms of enterprises, are Uttar Pradesh (44.03 lakh), West Bengal (36.64 lakh), Tamil Nadu (33.13 lakh), Maharashtra (30.63 lakh), Andhra Pradesh (25.96 lakh), Kerala (22.13 lakh), Gujarat (21.78 lakh), Karnataka (20.19 lakh), Madhya Pradesh (19.33 lakh) and Rajasthan (16.64 lakh).

The ten leading States, in terms of employment, are Uttar Pradesh (92.36 lakh), West Bengal (85.78 lakh), Tamil Nadu (80.98 lakh), Andhra Pradesh (70.69 lakh), Maharashtra (70.04 lakh), Kerala (49.62 lakh), Gujarat (47.73 lakh), Karnataka (46.72 lakh), Madhya Pradesh (33.66 lakh) and Odisha (33.24 lakh)

Table 2.2: State wise Distribution of Micro, Small and Medium Enterprise sector in India

(Figures in Lakhs)

Sl no	State/UTs	Registered Sector	Unregistered sector		Total
			Sample	Estimated 2005[*]	
1	Jammu & Kashmir	0.15	1.18	1.68	3.01
2	HimasalPradesh	0.12	1.6	1.16	2.87
3	Panjab	0.48	9.66	4.32	14.46
4	Chandigarh	0.01	0.28	0.2	0.49
5	Utarakhand0.242.001	0.24	2	1.5	3.74
6	Haryana	0.33	4.87	3.46	8.66
7	Delhi	0.04	1.75	3.74	5.52
8	Rajashan	0.5	59.1	46.96	16.6
9	Uttar Pradesh	1.88	22.34	19.82	44.03
10	Bihar	0.5	7.48	6.72	14.7
11	Sikkim	0	0.06	0.1	0.17
12	Arunachal Pradesh	0	0.25	0.15	0.41
13	Nagaland	0.01	0.16	0.21	0.39
14	Manipur	0.04	0.44	0.43	0.91
15	Mizram	0.04	0.1	0.16	0.29
16	Tripura	0.01	0.26	0.7	0.98
17	Meghalaya	0.03	0.47	0.38	0.88
18	Assam	0.20	2.14	4.28	6.62
19	West Bengal	0.43	20.8	13.41	34.64
20	Jharkhand	0.18	4.25	2.3	26.75
21	Odisha	0.2	9.77	5.76	15.73
22	Chhattisgarh	0.23	2.78	2.19	5.2
23	Madhya Pradesh	1.07	11.5	6.76	19.33
24	Gujarat	2.3	13.03	6.46	21.78
25	Daman &Diu	0.01	0.01	0.04	0.06
26	Dadra&Nagar Haveli	0.02	0.04	0.03	0.09
27	Maharashtra	0.87	14.45	15.31	30.63
28	Andra &Telungana	0.46	14.9	10.6	25.96
29	Karnataka	1.36	11.12	7.7	20.19
30	Goa	0.03	0.56	0.27	0.86
31	Lakshadweep	0	0.01	0.01	0.02
32	Kerala	1.5	12.94	7.69	22.13
33	Tamil Nadu	2.34	18.21	12.58	33.13
34	Puducherry	0.01	0.13	0.21	0.35
35	Andaman & Nicobar Ils.	0.01	0.07	0.07	0.14
	All India	15.64	198.74	147.38	361.76

Source: MSME Annual Report 2014-15, Government of India pp-27

The ten leading industries, in terms of enterprises, (as per National Industrial Classification 2004 at two digit level) are Retail Trade except of Motor Vehicles and Motorcycles; Repair of Personal and Household Goods (144.15 lakh), Manufacture of Wearing Apparel; Dressing and Dyeing of fur (31.65 lakh), Manufacture of Food Products and Beverages (25.12 lakh), Other Service Activities (22.43 lakh), Other Business Activities (13.64 lakh), Hotels and Restaurants (13.18 lakh), Sale, Maintenance and Repair of Motor Vehicles and Motorcycles; Retail Sale of Automotive Fuel (12.92 lakh), Manufacture of Furniture & Manufacturing not elsewhere classified (11.61 lakh), Manufacture of Fabricated Metal Products, except Machinery and Equipment (8.42 lakh), Manufacture of Textiles (8.42 lakh). The ten leading industries, in terms of employment, (as per National Industrial Classification 2004 at two digit level) are Retail Trade except of Motor Vehicles and Motorcycles; Repair of Personal and Household Goods (245.48 lakh), Manufacture of Food Products and Beverages (62.99 lakh), Manufacture of Wearing Apparel; Dressing and Dyeing (60.06 lakh), Other Service Activities (37.65 lakh), Manufacture of Textiles (35.91 lakh), Hotels and Restaurants (33.92 lakh), Sale, Maintenance & Repair of Motor Vehicles and Motorcycles; Retail Sale of Automotive Fuel (30.03 lakh), Manufacture of Furniture & Manufacturing not elsewhere classified (28.19 lakh), Other Business Activities (27.67 lakh), Education (27.26 lakh).

2.3.3. *Performance of Micro, Small & Medium Enterprises (MSME) Sector*

Table 2.3: Performance of MSME, Employment and Investments

S.No	Year	Total Working Enterprises (in Lakh)	Employment (in Lakh)	Market Value of Fixed Assets (Rs. in Crore)
I	II	III	IV	V
1.	2006-07	361.76	805.23	868,543.79
2.	2007-08	377.36	842.00	920,459.84
3.	2008-09	393.70	880.84	977,114.72
4.	2009-10	410.80	921.79	1,038,546.08
5.	2010-11	428.73	965.15	1,105,934.09
6.	2011-12	447.64	1,011.69	1,182,757.64
7.	2012-13	447.54	1,061.40	1.268,763.67
8.	2013-14	488.46	1,114.29	1,363,700.54

Source: The Final Report of the fourth all Indian census of small, micro enterprises 2006-2007: Government of India, pp -15

Performance of Micro, Small & Medium Enterprises (MSME) Sector is assessed by conduct of periodic All India Census of the Sector. The latest census conducted was Fourth All India Census of MSME. The Census was conducted with reference year 2006-07, wherein the data was collected till 2009 and results published in 2011-12. Fourth All India Census of MSME is the first census conducted post implementation of Micro, Small and Medium Enterprises Development (MSMED) Act, 2006, prior to implementation of MSMED Act, 2006.

2.3.4. *Contribution of MSME Sector in the Gross Domestic Product*

As per the revised methodology suggested by CSO, MoSPI, on the basis of the data on Gross Domestic Product (GDP) published by CSO, MoSPI and final results of the latest Census (Fourth Census), the estimated contribution of MSME sector to GDP and Output, during 2006-07 to 2012-13, are as noted below:

Table 2.4: Contribution of manufacturing Output of MSME in GDP (at 2004-05 prices)

Year	Gross Value of Output of MSME Manufacturing Sector (` in crore)	Share of MSME sector in total GDP (%)			Share of MSME Manufacturing output in total Manufacturing Output (%)
		Manufacturing Sector MSME	Services Sector MSME	Total	
2006-07	1198818	7.73	27.40	35.13	35.13
2007-08	1322777	7.81	27.60	35.41	35.41
2008-09	1375589	7.52	28.60	36.12	36.12
2009-10	1488352	7.45	28.60	36.05	36.05
2010-11	1653622	7.39	29.30	36.69	36.69
2011-12	1788584	7.27	30.70	37.97	37.97
2012-13	1809976	7.04	30.50	37.54	37.54

Source:
1. Fourth All India Census of MSME 2006-07,
2. National Accounts Statistics (2014), CSO, MOSPI and
3. Annual Survey of Industries, CSO MOSPI

2.4. Products and Services of MSMEs Sector

There are over 6000 products ranging from traditional to high-tech items, which are being manufactured by the MSME Sector in addition to provide wide range of services. Some important products are listed below

2.4.1. *Chemical & Plastic Items*

1. Agarbatti Sticks
2. Basic Dyes
3. Strand Board
4. Duplicating stencil paper

5. Liquid soaps

6. Paper Bags/envelopes

7. File covers, file Boards& Letter Paper

8. Gummed paper Tapes

9. HM/HDPE Bags

10. Fiber-glass Reinforced plastic products

11. Rubber Moulded Goods

12. Rigid PVC Pipes

13. Blow–Moulded Containers

14. Disposable Syringes

15. Injection Moulded plastic Items like

    i)   Office Trays

    ii) Calendar

    iii) Waste paper Baskets

    iv) Lunch Boxes

    v)   Sales & Paper Containers

16. Saline Glucose and Distilled Water for Injections

17. Special purpose paints

18. Nylon Buttons

19. Multi-layered CO-extruded Films

20. Audio- Video Cassettes

21. FRP furniture

22. PVC Covers, Folders, Bags.

23. Automobile Rubber Components, Shock Absorbers, Bushings, V-belts for Fan, Hoses and Tubes, Battery Tray, Mats and Matting's, Door Step etc.

24. Rubber Gloves, of various Varieties – Industrial Gloves, Household Gloves, Surgeon's Gloves, Electrician's Gloves.

25. Industrial Sheeting/Hospital Sheeting

26. Micro-cellular Rubber Sheets

27. HDPS/Polypropylene Box Strapping

28. Adhesives

2.4.2. *Food Industries*

1. Instant Food Mixes.
2. James, Jellies, Marmalade.
3. Fruit juices, nectars, beverages.
4. Ground & Processed Spices.
5. Pappads/Applams.
6. Pickle & condiments.
7. Oleoresins from chilies.
8. Mushroom cultivation.
9. Confectionary.
10. Soft ice cream.
11. Biscuits.
12. Peanut candy (groundnut & jiggery).
13. Macroni, spaghetti, etc.
14. Protein based beverages.
15. Dehydrated fruits and vegetables.

2.4.3. *Mechanical Products*

1. Printing press.
2. Automobile repairing/servicing.
3. Pilfer proof caps.
4. Wick stoves, nut an model.
5. Small springs.
6. Fabrication unit for making structural items like gates, grills etc.
7. Fountain fen nips.
8. Carts fitted with pneumatic tyres.
9. Aluminum builders hardware, TV stands, Antennas.
10. Drums up to 60 liters capacity.

2.4.4. *Metallurgy*

1. Ferrous Castings.
2. Non-ferrous Casting.

2.4.5. *Glass & Ceramic Industries*

1. Glass Pressed Wares viz. silica glass tumblers. Bowls, ashtrays.
2. Scientific laboratory glassware.
3. Building bricks.
4. Ophthalmic lenses.
5. Mosaic tiles.
6. Chalk crayons.
7. Simple glass mirrors.

2.4.6. *Cottage Industrial Products*

1. Areca nut cutting
2. Appalam manufacture.
3. Bee-keeping, agriculture, honey and bees wax.
4. Bakery, biscuits, cakes.
5. Bunco cakes.
6. Confectionary sweets.
7. Coffee roasting and grinding.
8. Dehydrate fruits and vegetables, dried fruits and dried vegetables.
9. Fruit canning.
10. Jiggery manufacture from Sugar-Cane, Date Palm or Palmyra and coconut tree, handmade Sugar, Sugar Candy.
11. Jam. Jelly's and preserves.
12. Syrups, Aerated water, ice making.
13. Vermicelli manufacture.
14. Apparel and readymade clothing (including sarees clothing).
15. Artificial flowers.
16. Aloe fiber extraction (Palmyra coconut fibers).
17. Banian manufacture.
18. Blanket weaving.
19. Block engraving for cloth printing.
20. Brush manufacture.
21. Button making out of mother of pearl, horns, brass and tin.
22. Calico printing.
23. Embroidery knitting and needle works.
24. Canvas shoes manufacture.

25. Hosiery with hand and power.

26. Laundry and cleaning cloths.

27. Leather goods making, books, shoes, chapels, slippers, bed straps.

28. Ornaments and jewellery (including bangles, combs).

29. Ornamental leather crafts, money purses, hand bags.

30. Weaving cotton, wool.

31. Spinning cotton, wool.

32. Tailoring.

33. Woolen fabric and woolen goods.

34. Wool clipping and grading.

35. Fly shutter loom making.

36. Ribbon manufacture.

37. Cane furniture (also cane and basket ware making).

38. Cement ware works.

39. Candle sticks manufacture.

40. Agar bathi making.

41. Manfr. Of cardboard and card board boxes.

42. Clay modeling.

43. Crayons.

44. Engraving on metals.

45. Enameling.

46. Handmade paper pulp, paper cutting and paper fans.

47. Inks, ink pads (for rubber stamps).

48. Lapidary work.

49. Musical instrument string or reed.

50. Painting on blanks glass.

51. Perfumery essential oils and scents.

52. Pith works-pith mat, garlands, flower.

53. Printing and allied trade, book binding, block making.

54. Soap making.

55. Korai mats, plates, blankets, hand bags, window screen.

56. Palmyra leaf, fancy and utility articles.

57. Palmyra rafters, stems, furniture, cost. making of cost and seating broom storm strips.

58. Palmyra fibre products.

59. Leans.

60. Match stick manufacturing (manufacture of splits with wood only).

61. Fountain manufacture.

62. Radio parts manufacture.

63. Braided cord manufacture.

64. Storing of articles in figidaries.

65. Toys.

66. Clips.

67. Decorticating dhal by hand grinding.

68. Twisting and winding of silk and cotton yarn.

69. Twisting and winding of silk thread, cotton thread and artificial yarn.

70. Wax coating on paper and cloth.

71. Power ghani.

72. Coconut leaf thatches making.

73. Beedi.

74. Plastic wire making to the furniture.

75. Pickles and mixture thatches making.

76. Pori making.

77. Basket making.

78. Brass and copper vessels making.

79. Country Bricks.

80. Rubber sheets.

81. Pottery.

82. Gem cutting.

83. Wet grain pounding.

84. Wiring for motor vehicles.

85. Photo and picture framing.

86. Silk cotton pillows and quits, and Coir, coir making rope.

2.4.7. *Handicrafts Industrial Products*

1. Carpets.
2. Hand printing.
3. Artistic textiles.
4. Embroidery & Zari Works.
5. Metal ware.
6. Jewellery.
7. Bagels and beads.
8. Conch shell.
9. Wood work.
10. Ceramics.
11. Stone Work.
12. Bamboo, Straw etc.
13. Flex Fiber.
14. Toys, dolls.
15. Paper machine.
16. Ivory Horn and Bone.
17. Leather.
18. Musical Instrument.
19. Incense and Perfumery.
20. Pottery.
21. Miscellaneous
22. Cumbly weaving.
    i. Cumbly weaving.
    ii. Palm- leaf articles.
    iii. Korai mats.
    iv. Date mats.
    v. Readymade Garments.
    vi. Cocoon Garlands.
    vii. Silverwares.
    viii. Aloe fiber.
    ix. Banana fiber products.

CHAPTER-III

INSTITUTIONAL SET UP FOR THE PROMOTION OF MICRO, SMALL & MEDIUM ENTERPRISES

3.1.   Introduction

Ministry of Micro, Small & Medium Enterprises (M/o MSME) is responsible for policy formulation, planning, development, export promotion and trade regulation of Small Scale industries in the country. This includes all kind of manpower, raw material, machineries and other inputs and sources that go into the production and marketing of goods and rendering services to end users. The vibrant MSME department is aiming to the growth and development of the MSME Sector, including Khadi, Village and Coir Industries, in cooperation with concerned Ministries/Departments, State Governments and other Stakeholders, through providing support to existing enterprises and encouraging creation of new enterprises. For this purpose, Ministry of Small Scale Industries and the Ministry of Agro and Rural Industries were merged to form the Ministry of Micro, Small and Medium Enterprises (M/o MSME). This Ministry now designs policies and promotes/facilitates programmes, projects and schemes and monitors their implementation with a view to assisting MSMEs and helps them to scale up.

The primary responsibility of promotion and development of MSMEs is of the State Governments. However, the Government of India, supplements efforts of the State Governments through various initiatives. The role of the ministry of MSME and its organisations is to assist the States in their efforts to encourage entrepreneurship, employment and livelihood opportunities and enhance the competitiveness of MSMEs in the changed economic scenario.

3.2.   Administrative Set up for MSMEs

The decentralised, scatted and labour intensive MSMEs are national levelly institutionalised through the Ministry of MSMEs which is headed by the Secretary, an Economic advisor and Development commissioners.

The administration system consists of following three structures.

1.   Setting up of Administrative and other supportive institutions.
2.   Implementation of sector development schemes and programmes.
3.   Legal and other Policy frame work.

3.2.1. *Administrative and other Supportive Institutions*

The Ministry of MSME is having two Divisions called Small & Medium Enterprises (SME) Wing and Agro & Rural Industry (ARI) Wing for the promotion and safeguard of small scale sector. (Table 3.1)

Table 3.1: Institutional Wings of Ministry of MSME

S.No	Name of the Mechanism	Objectives of the Mechanism
1.	Small & Medium Enterprises (SME) Wing	• The SME Wing is allocated the work, inter-alia, of administration, vigilance and administrative supervision of the National Small Industries Corporation (NSIC) Ltd., a public sector enterprise and the three autonomous national level entrepreneurship development/ training organizations. • The Wing is also responsible for implementation of the schemes relating to Performance and Credit Rating and Assistance to Training Institutions, among others. • SME Wing is also responsible for preparation and monitoring of Results-Framework Document (RFD) as introduced in 2009 by the Cabinet Secretariat under Performance Monitoring and Evaluation System (PMES).
2	Agro & Rural Industry (ARI) Wing.	Administration of the • Khadi and Village Industries Commission (KVIC), • Coir Board • Mahatma Gandhi Institute for Rural Industrialisation (MGIRI). • The implementation of the Prime Minister's Employment Generation Programme (PMEGP).

Source: Compiled from Secondary Data

3.2.2. *The Micro, Small and Medium Enterprises–Development Organisation (MSME-DO) [Earlier known as SIDO]*

The Micro, Small and Medium Enterprises-Development Organisation (MSME-DO) [earlier known as SIDO], headed by the Special Secretary & Development Commissioner (MSME), being an apex body for formulating and overseeing implementation of the policies for the development of MSMEs in the country, is playing a very positive and constructive role for strengthening this vital sector.

Table 3.2: Role of the Micro, Small and Medium Enterprises–Development Organisation

S.No	Name of the Mechanism	Objectives of the Mechanism
1.	Net work Function (with other organisation)	• MSME- District Industrial Centre • Regional Testing Centre • Footwear Training Institutes • Production Centre • Field Testing Stations and • specialized institutes
2	Promotional and other developmental services	• Advising the Government in Policy formulation for the promotion and development of MSMEs • Providing techno-economic and managerial consultancy, common facilities and extension services to MSME units. • Providing facilities for technology up gradation, modernization, quality improvement and infrastructure. • Developing Human Resources through training and skill up gradation. • Providing economic information services. • Maintaining a close liaison with the Central Ministries, Planning Commission, State Governments, Financial Institutions and other Organisations concerned with development of MSMEs. • Evolving and coordinating Policies and Programmes for development of MSMEs as ancillaries to large and medium scale industries.

Source: Compiled from Secondary Data

Micro, Small and Medium Enterprises–Development Organisation acts as a policy formulating, co-ordinating and monitoring agency for the development of small scale industries at National level. It provides a wide range of extension services through its network of 27 Small Industries Service Institutes, 31 Branch Small Industries Service Institutes (SISIs), 37 SISI Extension centres, 4 Regional Testing Centres. 19 Field Testing Stations, 3 Product cum process Development Centres, 2 Central Foot wear training Centres, 2 central Tool Rooms, I central Institute of Hand Tools and 4 production Centres (two of them are also working as extension centres). Each of these institutes is fully equipped with technical officers, workshop and testing facilities to provide technical and other assistance to small scale units in the area of their location. (Table 3.2)

There are 77 common facility workshops attached to SISIs/ Branch SISIs. Extension centres have workshop facilities for technical disciplines like General Engineering, Tool Room, and Heat treatment, Electroplating, Glass and Ceramics, Forging, Chemical Labs etc. MSME-DO through its network of field officers helps small-scale units by providing marketing counselling, consultancy services and conducting product oriented market surveys

a) Economic Information

Industry prospect sheets, area survey reports, project profiles, feasibility studies/reports are brought out by MSME-DO which provide information on the scope for development of various industries.

b) Technical Assistance

MSME-DO provides technical consultancy on the manufacture of technical processes, use of modern machines and equipments, preparation of designs, lay-ot of machinery and assistance on all aspects of production.

c) Quality Improvement and Testing

With a view to improving the quality of the products being manufactured in the small scale sector, 4 Regional Testing Centres have been set up at New Delhi, Bombay, Calcutta and Madras. In addition, there are 19 Field Testing Stations in areas of concentration of specific groups of industries to provide specialized testing facilities for a particular product or industry group.

d) Industrial Management & Training

MSME-DO offers consultancy services in the field of techno management, marketing, quality control, production, finance, labour laws etc., and undertakes special training programmes, in plant studies, open house discussions and seminars. Institute- wise panel management experts etc., is maintained by the SISIs with a view to supplement consultancy services and training facilities provided by SIDO. Small scale units can utilize the services of these consultants which are available at subsidized rates.

3.2.3. *National Small Industries Corporation (NSIC), New Delhi*

The National Small Industries Corporation was established in 1955 with the view to assist. Promote, develop and finance small scale industries in the country. The main functions of the corporation are:

a) To secure Government orders for the small industries
b) To provide loans
c) To provide technical assistance
d) To secure Co-ordination between small-scale and large scale industries, so that the former produce goods required by the latter and,
e) To underwrite and guarantee loans from banks and other sources.

Apart from providing finance, the corporation has rendered valuable service in the field of supply of machinery on hire–purchases system to the small industries and in securing government orders for small industrial units.

The NSIC has its regional offices at Delhi, Calcutta, Bombay, Madras & Gauhati, and branches in the southern zone at Bangalore, Hyderabad, Pondicherry, Coimbatore, Cochin & Trissur. There is a Computer training centre at Tenkasi, Tirunelveli District in Tamil Nadu and Marketing development centres at Madras & Cochin.

3.2.4. *Technical Consultancy Organisations (TCOs)*

Provision of appropriate and inexpensive consultancy services to small and new entrepreneurs is a pre-requisite for achieving wider geographical dispersal of small and medium enterprises all over the county. For this purpose, Technical consultancy organizations (TCOs) were set up in the early 1970s and early 80s. IDBI, IFCI and ICICI in collaboration with state level financial/development institutions and commercial banks established a net-work of TCO's. There are 18 TCOs in the country, some of them covering more than one state. TCO's have been set up to provide a package of total consultancy services to state governments, state-level development financing institutions and banks. The major thrust of TCO's operations is in the area of preparation of project reports and feasibility studies. Having gained experience over the years, TCOs have diversified into the field of identification of potential entrepreneurs and their training, project implementation, rehabilitation, management consultancy, detailed design engineering and turn-key services besides energy audit and conservation.

3.2.5. Khadi & Village Industries Commission (KVIC)

The Khadi & Village Industries Commission (KVIC), established under the Khadi and Village Industries Commission Act, 1956, is a statutory organisation engaged in promoting and developing khadi and village industries for providing employment opportunities in rural areas, thereby strengthening the rural economy. The KVIC has been identified as one of the major organisations in the decentralized sector for generating sustainable rural non-farm employment opportunities at low per capita investment. This also helps in checking migration of rural population to urban areas in search of the employment opportunities.

3.2.6. Mahatma Gandhi Institute for Rural Industrialisation(MGIRI)

The national level institute namely 'Mahatma Gandhi Institute for Rural Industrialization (MGIRI)" (erstwhile Jamnalal Bajaj Central Research Institute) has been established as a society under Societies (Registration) Act, 1860 at Wardha, Maharashtra, to strengthen the R&D activities in KVI sector. The main functions of the Institute are to improve the R&D activities under rural industrial sector through encouraging research, extension of R&D, quality control, training and dissemination of technology related information.

3.2.7. Coir Board

The Coir Board is a statutory body established under the Coir Industry Act, 1953 for promoting overall sustainable development of the coir industry and improving the living conditions of the workers engaged in this traditional industry. The activities of the Board for development of coir industries, inter-alia, include undertaking scientific, technological and economic research and development activities; developing new products & designs; and marketing of coir and coir products in India and abroad. It also promotes co-operative organisations among producers of husks, coir fibre, coir yarn and manufacturers of coir products; ensuring remunerative returns to producers and manufacturers, etc. The Board has promoted two research institutes namely; Central Coir Research Institute (CCRI), Kalavoor, Alleppey, and Central Institute of Coir Technology (CICT), Bengaluru for undertaking research and development activities on different aspects of coir industry, which is one of the major agro based rural industries in the country.

3.2.8. National Entrepreneurship Development Institutes

Entrepreneurship development and training is one of the key elements for the promotion of micro, small and medium enterprises (MSMEs), especially for creation of new enterprises by the first generation entrepreneurs. In order to inculcate the entrepreneurial culture amongst the first generation of entrepreneurs on a regular basis, the Ministry has set up three national level Entrepreneurship Development Institutes viz;

- *The National Institute for Entrepreneurship and Small Business Development (NIESBUD)* (1983) at NOIDA (Uttar Pradesh),
- *National Institute for Micro, Small and Medium Enterprises (NI-MSME)* (1960) at Hyderabad, and
- *Indian Institute of Entrepreneurship (IIE)* (1993) at Guwahati, as autonomous societies.

These institutes are engaged in developing training modules; undertaking research & training; and providing consultancy services for entrepreneurship development & promotion of MSMEs, including enhancement of their competitiveness.

3.2.9. National Board for Micro, Small and Medium Enterprises (NB MSME)

The range of development work in MSMEs involves several Departments/ Ministries and different organisations of Central/State Governments. To facilitate coordination and inter-institutional linkages and in pursuance of the MSME Development Act, 2006, a National Board for Micro, Small & Medium Enterprises consisting of a total of 47 members has been constituted with 20 non-official members. It is an apex advisory body constituted to pertaining to the MSME sector. The Minister In charge of MSME of the Government of India is the Chairman and the Board comprises among others, State Industry Ministers, some Members of Parliament, Secretaries of various Departments of Government of India, financial institutions, public sector undertakings, industry associations and eminent experts in the field. The board meets periodically to take stock of the issues pertaining to policy matters.

3.3. Micro, Small and Medium Enterprises Development Schemes and Programmes

Both the Central and State Governments of India are urging to implement various MSMEs development schemes and make an intervention into this sector through implementation of its schemes for the up gradation of this sector

3.3.1. National level Development Schemes

1. Credit Linked Capital Subsidy Scheme (CLCSS)

The Ministry of Micro, Small and Medium Enterprises (MSME) is operating a Scheme namely Credit Linked Capital Subsidy Scheme (CLCSS) for Technology Up gradation of Micro and Small Enterprises. The Scheme aims at facilitating Technology Up gradation of Micro and Small Enterprises (earlier known as Small Scale Industries). The Scheme was launched in October 2000 and revised from 29.09.2005. The revised scheme aims at facilitating Technology Up gradation of Micro and Small Enterprises by providing 15% Capital Subsidy (limited to maximum Rs. 15.00 lakh) for purchase of Plant & Machinery. Maximum limit of eligible loan for calculation of subsidy under the scheme is Rs.100 lakh. Presently, more than 1500 technologies under 51 products /sub-sectors have been approved under the scheme. Since inception of the scheme, 30,732 units have availed subsidy of Rs. 1776.58 crores till 31.12.2014.

2. Credit Guarantee Fund Scheme for Micro and Small Enterprises

The Government launched the Credit Guarantee Fund Scheme for Small Industries (now renamed as Credit Guarantee Fund Scheme for Micro and Small Enterprises) in August, 2000 with the objective of making available credit to MSEs, particularly Micro Enterprises, for loans up to Rs. 100 lakh without collateral/ third party guarantees. The scheme is being operated by the Credit Guarantee Fund Trust for Micro and Small Enterprises (CGTMSE) set up jointly by the Government of India and SIDBI. The scheme is being operated by the Credit Guarantee Fund Trust for Micro and Small Enterprises (CGTMSE) set up jointly by the Government of India and SIDBI.

At present 133 eligible lending institutions registered as MLIs of the Trust comprising of 26 Public Sector banks, 20 Private Sector Banks, 73 Regional Rural Banks (RRBs), 4 foreign banks and 9 other Institutions ViZ. Delhi Finance Corporation, Kerala Financial Corporation, Jammu & Kashmir Development Corporation Ltd, Andhara Pradesh State Financial Corporation, Export Import Bank of India, The Tamil Nadu Industrial Investment Corporation Ltd. , National Small Industries Corporation(NSIC), North Eastern Development Finance Corporation(NEDFI) and Small Industries Development Bank of India(SIDBI). As on 31st December 2014, cumulatively 17, 22,488 proposals have been approved for guarantee cover for a total sanctioned loan amount of Rs. 85,607.35 crore

3. *Scheme of Micro Finance Programme*

The Ministry has been operating a Scheme of Micro Finance Programme since 2003-04 which has been tied up with the existing Micro Credit Scheme of SIDBI. Under the Scheme, the Government of India provides funds to SIDBI under 'Portfolio Risk Fund' requirements of loan from the MFIs/NGOs. At present SIDBI takes fixed deposit equal to 10% of the loan amount. Under the PRF, the share of MFIs/NGOs is 2.5% of the loan amount (i.e. 25% of security deposit) and balance 7.5% (i.e. 75% of security deposit) is adjusted from the funds provided by the Government under the scheme. The funds under PRF are to be utilized for extending loans in the underserved States like North Eastern States including Sikkim, Bihar, Jharkhand, West Bengal, Orissa, Madhya Pradesh, Chhattisgarh, Uttar Pradesh, Jammu & Kashmir, Rajasthan and Uttarakhand and underserved pockets/ districts of other States. As on 31st December 2014, Cumulative loan amount provided to MFIs/NGOs under the scheme stood at Rs 2199.11 crore covering approximately 27.19 lakh beneficiaries.

4. *Micro & Small Enterprises Cluster Development Programme (MSE-CDP)*

The Micro and Small Enterprises – Cluster Development Programme (MSE-CDP) is being implemented for holistic and integrated development of micro and small enterprises in clusters through Soft Interventions (such as diagnostic study, capacity building, marketing development, export promotion, skill development, technology up gradation, organizing workshops, seminars, training, study visits, exposure visits, etc.), Hard Interventions (setting up of Common Facility Canters) and Infrastructure Up gradation(create/upgrade infrastructural facilities in the new/existing industrial areas/clusters of MSEs).

Table 3.3: National level MSMEs Development Schemes

S.No	Name of the Scheme	Year of starting	Objectives of this scheme
1	Credit Linked Capital Subsidy Scheme (CLCSS)	October.2002	Facilitating Technology Up gradation of Micro and Small Enterprises by providing 15% Capital Subsidy (limited to maximum Rs. 15.00 lakh) for purchase of Plant & Machinery.
2	Guarantee Fund Trust for Micro and Small Enterprises	August, 2000	Credit facility to MSEs, particularly Micro Enterprises, for loans up to Rs. 100 lakh without collateral/ third party guarantees.
3	Scheme of Micro Finance Programme	2003-04	GoI provides funds to SIDBI under 'Portfolio Risk Fund' requirements of loan from the MFIs/NGOs.
4	The Micro and Small Enterprises – Cluster Development Programme	2003-04	Cluster level Government Soft Interventions and Hard Interventions (setting up of Common Facility Canters) and Infrastructure Up gradation (create/upgrade infrastructural facilities in the new/existing industrial areas/ clusters of MSEs).
5	National Manufacturing Competitiveness Programme	2007-08	Providing Support for "Entrepreneurial and Managerial Development of SMEs through Incubators"
6	Scheme for "Building Awareness on Intellectual Property Rights" (IPR) for MSMEs	11th Five-Year	Enhancing awareness of MSMEs about Intellectual Property Rights (IPRs) for taking measures for protecting their ideas and business strategies
7	Lean Manufacturing Competitiveness Scheme for MSMEs	2009-10	Application of Lean Manufacturing(LM) techniques like 5S system, visual control, standard operating procedures(SOPs), just in time(JIT), KANBAN system, cellular layout, value stream Mapping, POKA Yoke, single Minutes Exchange of Dies(SMED), Total Productive, Kaizen Blitz.
8	Enabling Manufacturing Sector to be Competitive through Quality Management Standards (QMS) and Quality Technology Tools (QTT)"	11th Five-Year	Improving the quality of the products in the MSME sector and inculcating the quality consciousness in enterprises in this sector.
9	Marketing Assistance and Technology Up gradation Scheme for MSMEs	11th Five-Year	Enhancing MSME's competitiveness in the National as well as International market through various activities such as Technology up gradation in Packaging, Skills up gradation/Development for Modern Marketing Techniques, Competition Studies of threatened products, Special components for North Eastern Region (NER)
10	Design Clinics scheme for MSMEs	XII Plan	Bringing the MSME sector and design expertise on a common platform and to provide expert advice and solutions on real time design problems, resulting in new product development, continuous improvement and value-addition .
11	Promotion of Information & Communication Tools (ICT) in MSME Sector	XII Plan	Motivating MSMEs to adopt ICT tools and applications in their production & business processes with a view to improve marketing competitiveness.
12	ISO-9000/ISO-14001/HACCP Certification Reimbursement Scheme		Reimbursement of charges for acquiring ISO 9000/14001/HACCP certification in MSEs to the extent of 75% of the cost subject to the maximum of Rs.75000/-.
13	SSI-MDA Scheme: Participation in Overseas International Trade Fairs/Exhibitions	XII Plan	Providing assistance under Marketing Development Assistance Scheme to MSEs for getting exposure and to export to the international markets through participation in overseas International Trade Fairs
14	Bar Code Scheme	XII Plan	SSI-MDA Scheme has the provision for reimbursement of 75% of one-time registration fees and annual recurring fees (for first three years) for adoption of Bar Code.

Source: Compiled from Secondary Data

Assistance is Provided for the Following Activities Under the Scheme

1. Preparation of Diagnostic Study Report with Government of India (GoI) grant of maximum Rs 2.50 lakh.
2. Soft Interventions with GoI grant of 75% of the sanctioned amount of the maximum project cost of Rs 25.00 lakh per cluster. For NE & Hill States, Clusters with more than 50% (a) micro/ village (b) women owned (c) SC/ST units, the GoI grant will be 90%.
3. Detailed Project Report (DPR) with GoI grant of maximum Rs 5.00 lakh for preparation of a technical feasibility and viability project report.
4. Hard Interventions in the form of tangible assets like Common Facility Centre having machinery and equipment for critical processes, research and development, testing, etc. with GoI grant up to 70% of the cost of project of maximum Rs 15.00 crore.
5. Infrastructure Development with GoI grant of upto 60% of the cost of project of Rs 10.00 crore, excluding cost of land. GoI grant will be 80% for projects in NE & Hill States, industrial areas/ Estates with more than 50% (a) micro (b) women owned (c) SC/ST units.

The GoI assistance shall also be available to Associations of Women Entrepreneurs for establishing exhibition centres at central places for display and sale of products of women owned micro and small enterprises @ 40% of the project cost.

5. *National Manufacturing Competitiveness Programme (NMCP)*

The National Manufacturing Competitiveness Programme (NMCP) is the nodal programme of the Government of India to develop global competitiveness among Indian MSMEs. Conceptualised by the National Manufacturing Competitiveness Council (NMCC), the Programme was initiated in 2007-08 with Providing Support for "Entrepreneurial and Managerial Development of SMEs through Incubators" The Office of DC (MSME) has selected 138 Business incubators for implementing the above scheme and released Rs. 15.848 Crore (*Table -3.3*).

Table 3.3: Year wise progress of National Manufacturing Competitiveness Programme

Year	No of Incubator selected/approved	No of Innovative Ideas selected/ approved	Total funds Provided / released. (Rs. in Crore)
2008-09	25	18	-
2009-10	29	164	1.906
2010-11	22	95	5.76
2011-12	-	49	2.06
2012-13	26	29	2.301
2013-14	16	53	2.506
2014-15	20	95	1.3218
Total	138	503	15.8548

Source; MSMEs Annual Report 2014-15, Government of India pp-244

6. Scheme for "Building Awareness on Intellectual Property Rights" (IPR) for the Micro, Small & Medium Enterprises (MSME)

The objective of the scheme is to enhance awareness of MSMEs about Intellectual Property Rights (IPRs) for taking measures for protecting their ideas and business strategies. Accordingly, to enable the MSME sector to face the challenges of liberalisation, various activities on IPR are being implemented under this scheme. These initiatives will provide MSME sector more information, orientation and facilities for protecting their intellectual property.

Table 3.4: List of Activities for Assistance provided under the scheme of Building Awareness on Intellectual Property Rights" (IPR) for the Micro, Small & Medium Enterprises

S.No	Activities for assistance	Assistant provided as on 2014-15
1	Awareness/ Sensitisation Programmes,	278Awareness/ Sensitisation Programmes
2	Pilot Studies for Selected Clusters/ Groups of Industries,	One Pilot Study was conducted on Cane and Bamboo
3	Interactive Seminars / Workshops,	88 Workshops / Seminars and 7 Short Term Training Programmes
4	Assistance for Grant on Patent/ GI Registration	Financial assistance was released to one unit for Grant of Patent.
5	Setting up of 'IP Facilitation Centre	setting up of 28 Intellectual Property Facilitation Centres (IPFCs)
6	Interaction with International Agencies	WIPO, Geneva
7	Public-Private Partnership	

Source: Compiled from Secondary Data

7. *Lean Manufacturing Competitiveness Scheme for MSMEs*

Lean Technologies are important in achieving Zero defect and Zero effect manufacturing. The share of manufacturing sector in Indian National GDP over the years has decreased to 14%. National Manufacturing policy of Government of India envisages share of manufacturing to reach target of 25% of the National GDP by 2022 also vision by New National Programme- "Make in India". The Lean Manufacturing Scheme(LMCS) is basically a business to enhance competitiveness of the manufacturing sector, imbibing a culture of continuous improvement, inculcating good management system resulted through increase in overall productivity, quality of the product, process improvement, cost reduction, scientific inventory management, improved process flows, reduced engineering time and so on with the application of Lean Manufacturing(LM) techniques like 5S system, visual control, standard operating procedures(SOPs), just in time(JIT), KANBAN system, cellular layout, value stream Mapping, POKA Yoke, single Minutes Exchange of Dies(SMED), Total Productive, Kaizen Blitz.

The lean Manufacturing Competitiveness Scheme was stared as a pilot phase in 2009 for 100 Mini clusters (10 or so manufacturing MSME units) in 11th Five year Plan. National Productivity Council (NPC) was selected as National Monitoring and Implementing Unit (NMIU) for facilitating implementation and monitoring of the scheme. Intervention of Lean Techniques stated in 89 clusters and successfully Work completed in 59 Mini Clusters with expenditure of Rs. 16.0 crore under the Pilot phase of LMCS. The brief progress details of the Pilot Phase are as below:

Table 3.5: List of Activities of Lean Manufacturing Competitiveness Scheme for MSMEs

Activities	Target (Nos.)	Achievement
Awareness Programmes covering 138 mini clusters	100	120
SPVs/DPGs formed	100	112
SPVs/DPGs functioning	100	99
LMC Selected	100	94
Tripartite agreement signed	100	89
Completed Mini Clusters	100	59

Source: Compiled from Secondary Data

The success and need of the scheme was evaluated (2012) by independent body i.e by Quality Council of India (QCI). The evaluation report on implementation of Pilot LMCS has recommended the continuation of the Scheme keeping in view benefits amounting to about 20% increased in productivity to the units. Following are the few clippings of photograph showing differences before and after the status of implementation of the scheme.

8. *Enabling Manufacturing Sector to be Competitive through Quality Management Standards (QMS) and Quality Technology Tools (QTT)*

The scheme, "Enabling Manufacturing Sector to be Competitive through Quality Management Standards (QMS) and Quality Technology Tools (QTT)" is aimed at improving the quality of the products in the MSME sector and inculcating the quality consciousness in enterprises in this sector. This Scheme was implemented during 11th Five-Year. After evaluation study the scheme is being conducted during the 12th Five Year Plan.

Table 3.6: List of Activities to Enabling Manufacturing Sector to be Competitive through Quality Management Standards (QMS) and Quality Technology Tools (QTT)

S.No	Activities for assistance	Assistant provided as on 2014-15
1	Introduction of Appropriate Modules for Technical Institutions	Course Module for the polytechnic prepared by QCI has been accepted by Ministry of HRD.
2	Organizing Awareness Campaigns for MSEs	578 Nos. of awareness programmes have been conducted
3	Organizing Competition-Watch (C-Watch);	
4	Implementation of Quality Management Standards and Quality Technology Tools in selected MSME	The DSR of 10 cluste rs/ 100 units have been prepared and implementation of QMS/QTT in these units is in the final stage.
5	Training programmes and Workshops	1800 Nos. ITI teachers have been trained on QMS/QTT by Quality Council of India (QCI). Two International study missions to Japan have been organized)

Source: Compiled from Secondary Data

9. *Technology and Quality Up gradation Support to MSMEs:*

The objective of this component of NMCP is to sensitize the MSMEs about the benefits that could accrue from usage of energy efficient technologies, reduction in emissions of Green House Gases, improve the acceptance of their products by product quality certification, thereby making them globally competitive.

Table 3.7: List of Activities of Technology and Quality Up gradation Supportive Scheme to MSMEs

S.No	Activities for assistance	Assistant provided as on 2014-15
1	Capacity Building of MSME Clusters for Energy Efficiency/Clean Development Interventions	Awareness programmes are implemented
2	Implementation of Energy Efficient Technologies in MSME sector	56 nos. of units have been approved by the Scheme Steering Committee (SSC) for assistance towards implementing energy efficient technology during the current
3	Encouraging MSMEs to acquire product certification licenses from National / International bodies.	67 nos. of Product Certification have been reimbursements

Source: Compiled from Secondary Data

10. Marketing Assistance and Technology Up gradation Scheme for MSMEs

The objective of this scheme is to enhance MSME's competitiveness in the National as well as International market through various activities such as Technology up gradation in Packaging, Skills up gradation/Development for Modern Marketing Techniques, Competition Studies of threatened products, Special components for North Eastern Region (NER), Identification of new markets through state/district level, local exhibitions/trade fairs, Corporate Governance Practices, Marketing Hubs and Reimbursement to ISO 18000/ 22000/ 27000 Certification. In this Connection, Targets have been allotted to MSME-DIs for participation of MSME units in the domestic exhibitions/fairs, reimbursement for ISO 18000/ 22000/27000 certification and for Corporate Governance Practices. Financial assistance of Rs. 340.59 lakhs has been providing to 2464 MSME units benefitted under the Scheme up to 31.12.2014.

11. Design Clinics scheme for MSMEs

The main objective of this component is to bring the MSME sector and design expertise on a common platform and to provide expert advice and solutions on real time design problems, resulting in new product development, continuous improvement and value-addition for existing products. It also aims at value-added cost effective solutions. National Institute of Design (NID) Ahmedabad is working as nodal agency

Table 3.8: List of Activities of Design Clinics Scheme for MSMEs

S.No	Activities for assistance	Assistant provided as on 2014-15
1	organizing seminars	156 seminars have been organized
2	Organizing workshops in MSME clusters	53 Nos. of Design Awareness workshops were also conducted.
3	Designing projects of MSME units	90 Nos. Design Projects received from MSME units for design intervention approved by the Government for financial assistance

Source: Compiled from Secondary Data

12. Promotion of Information & Communication Tools (ICT) in MSME Sector

The main objective of the scheme is to motivate MSMEs to adopt ICT tools and applications in their production & business processes with a view to improve their competitiveness in national & International market. The likely development outcomes of the scheme will be:

- To promote an echo system of cost effective and all inclusive ICT applications for MSMEs through Cloud Computing
- To establish Inter and Intra Networks amongst Technology Centers and Institutions of Office of DC, MSME
- To enable MSMEs to search for value chain (raw material, experts) online
- Adoption of best practices to improve quality of products and services
- Reducing delivery cycle time
- IT as a medium of communication to revamp access to the markets, enhanced access empowers the market to undertake direct, faster and better transactions.
- Evolving internal efficiencies by way of intense ICT intake and automating procedure for cost reduction and capacity enhancement for information access, processing, collaboration and dissemination.

13. ISO-9000/ISO-14001/HACCP Certification Reimbursement Scheme

The scheme envisages one time reimbursement of charges for acquiring ISO 9000/14001/ HACCP certification in MSEs to the extent of 75% of the cost subject to the maximum of Rs.75000/-. An amount of Rs 132.11 Crore has been reimbursed to 25,652 units since inception of the Scheme till 31st March, 2014. During 2014-15 about 74 Lakh to 125 units has been reimbursed upto 31st December 2014.

14. SSI-MDA Scheme: Participation in Overseas International Trade Fairs/ Exhibitions

GoI has been providing assistance under Marketing Development Assistance Scheme to MSEs for getting exposure to the international markets and exploring possibility of export of their products by exhibiting them through participation in overseas International Trade Fairs. During 2014-15, Office of DC (MSME) has participated in 13 International Trade Fairs in which 195 units has participated. Total expenditure till 16.12.2014 is Rs. 1.97 crore.

15. Bar Code Scheme

SSI-MDA Scheme has the provision for reimbursement of 75% of one-time registration fees and annual recurring fees (for first three years) paid by Micro and Small Enterprise (MSEs) to GS1 India for adoption of Bar Code. The scheme aims at enhancing marketing competitiveness of MSEs. Financial assistance of Rs. 62, 43,049 lakhs has been provided to 387 MSEs Upto 31st December 2014 for reimbursement of one-time registration fees and annual recurring fees.

3.4.   Development Porgrammes for MSMEs

1. District Industries Centres (DICs)

The District Industries Centres Programme was launched in 1978 throughout the country to help in effective development of small, tiny and cottage industries all over the country, including, rural and backward areas. This programme was launched with the objective of providing a package of assistance needed for setting up small, cottage and tiny industries with greater emphasis on maximum generation of employment, and all services and support facilities. Now there are 422 District industries centres established throughout the country. They provide requisite service and support assistance to the entrepreneur in the form of technical guidance, project reports and help in getting the credit and other essential inputs.

2. Entrepreneurial Development Programmes

The Entrepreneurial Development programmes and creation of awareness in people towards setting up of small scale industries are two important prerequisites for industrial development and reduction of unemployment. A number of Entrepreneurial Development programmes are, therefore, being organized by SIDO through small industries service institutes (SISIs) and their branches, since 1970, with the help of Stat Directorates of Industries, State Financial Corporations, Commercial Banks and other Developmental Agencies for the benefit of different target groups, consisting of both skilled/semiskilled and educated/ uneducated persons. These programmes are organized for engineering and non-engineering entrepreneurs.

Entrepreneurial Development Programmes for non-engineers include women, rural artisans, and technicians, weaker sections of the society, educated unemployed and the physically handicapped.

3.   *Ancillary Development and Sub-contracting Exchanges*

Under the Ancillary Development Programme, individual items are identified for ancillarisation and small scale industries are assisted for securing sub-contract jobs with a view to providing them effective marketing support. As a part of this programme, 16 Sub-Contracting Exchanges have been set up in SISIs to promote ancillarisation. These exchanges act as an information house for matching the requirements of medium/large undertakings looking for sub contractors with small scale units desirous of securing orders from medium/large undertakings.

4.   *Modernisation Programmes*

The Modernisation programme envisages up gradation of obsolete technology of MSMEs though identification of their input needs in rural, urban and backward areas of the country. The main objectives of the programme are:

1.   Improvement in production technology
2.   Product Development Design
3.   Testing, Design and Quality Control
4.   Machinery and equipment
5.   Selection of proper raw material
6.   Application of improved management technology.

Under the Modernisation programme, seminars, industrial clinics, industrial workshops, modernization course and study visits are organised. 20 industries have been selected on All India basis and 38 industries on concentration basis in different States.

5.   *Government Stores Purchase Programme*

The National Small Industries Corporation verifies the competence of small scale units for executing government orders and enlists them for participation in Government Stores purchase programme. 409 items are reserved for exclusive purchase from MSMEs units/KVIC/Women Development Corporations by the government purchasing agencies. A price preference extending up to 15% is given to small scale units over medium/large scale units.

6. *Reservation of Items for Production*

With a view to giving protection to MSMEs, particular articles have been reserved exclusively. (Table 3.9)

Table 3.9: List of Items Reserved for Exclusive MSMES Sector

S.No.	Product Code	Name of the Product		
20-21		**Food and Allied Industries**		
1	3	202501	Pickles & chutneys	
2	7	205101	Bread	
3	11	21100102	Mustard Oil (except solvent extracted)	
4	13	21100104	Ground nut oil (except solvent extracted)	
27		**Wood and Wood Products**		
5	47	276001	Wooden furniture and fixtures	
28		**PAPER PRODUCTS**		
6	79	285002	Exercise books and registers	
30-31		**Other Chemicals and Chemical Products**		
7	253	305301	Wax candles	
8	308	314201	Laundry soap	
9	313	317001	Safety matches	
10	314	318401	Fire works	
11	319	319902	Agarbatties	
32		**Glass & Ceramics**		
12	335	321701	Glass bangles	
34		**Mechanical engg. Excluding transport equipment**		
13	364	340101	Steel admiral	
14	394	341004	Rolling shutters	
15	402	34200602	Steel chairs-All types	
16	404	34200702	Steel tables-All other types	
17	409	342099	Steel furniture-All other types	
18	428	343302	Padlocks	
19	447A	345207	Stainless steel utensils	
20	474	345202	Domestic utensils-Aluminium	

Source: MSMEs Annual Report -2014-15, Government of India pp-244

7. *Awards for MSMEs' Entrepreneurs*

In order to encourage the entrepreneurs and give them proper recognition in MSME industries, a scheme for national award has been introduced since 1983-84. (Table 3.10)

Table 3.10: List of National Awards to MSMEs

S.No	Name of the Award	Prize /No's
1	Outstanding performance in Entrepreneurship, Research and Development, Innovation, Lean Manufacturing Techniques and Quality Products.	1. First - Rs.3, 00,000/-, 2. Second- Rs.2, 00,000/- 3. Third - Rs.1, 50,000/-
	Special Award to 1. Outstanding Woman entrepreneur 2. Outstanding entrepreneur form SC/ST 3. Entrepreneur from North Eastern Region	 One number One number One number
2	National Awards for Research & Development Efforts in Micro, Small and Medium Enterprises	Three awards one each in micro, small and medium enterprises categories
3	National Award for Innovation in Micro, Small and Medium Enterprises (MSMEs)	Three awards one each in micro, small and medium enterprises categories
4	Outstanding Entrepreneurship Efforts in Micro, Small and Medium Enterprises (MSMEs)	Three awards one each in micro, small and medium enterprises categories
5	National Award for Quality Products in Micro & Small Enterprises (MSEs) (1) Essential oil and perfumery products (2) Bio-Technology Products (3) Hand Tools (4) Builders Hardware (5) Electrical Home Appliances (6) Electro- Medical Instruments/ Equipments (7) Glass Tableware Products (8) Bakery Products.	One National Award is given for each category for the selected products
6	National Awards for Lean Manufacturing Techniques	Three awards one each in micro, small and medium enterprises categories
7	National Awards to Banks for Excellence in MSE Lending and Excellence in Lending to Micro Enterprises.	

The awards are given to MSMEs for outstanding performance in Entrepreneurship, Research and Development, Innovation, Lean Manufacturing Techniques and Quality Products. The First, Second and Third National Awards carry a cash prize of Rs.3,00,000/-, Rs.2,00,000/- and Rs.1,50,000/- respectively, a certificate and a trophy. Selection for awards is made on the basis of a set criteria exclusively designed to evaluate performance of the MSMEs. Under the scheme, an exhibition is also organized for MSMEs during the India International Trade Fair (IITF) at Pragati Maiden to exhibit and explore the market potential of the products manufactured by MSMEs/National Awardees.

National Award for Research & Development efforts in Micro, Small and Medium Enterprises (MSMEs)

National Awards for Research & Development Efforts in Micro, Small and Medium Enterprises are given for encouraging in-house R&D efforts and promoting this spirit in the larger interest of qualitative development in MSME Sector. Under this Scheme, three awards each for Micro and Small Enterprises and for Medium Enterprises were conferred upon deserving registered MSMEs.

National Award for Innovation in Micro, Small and Medium Enterprises (MSMEs)

These Awards have been included from the last year. This category includes three First Awards, one in each category for Micro, Small & Medium Enterprises and these awards have been gone to entrepreneurs from Delhi, Haryana and Punjab respectively.

Outstanding Entrepreneurship Efforts in Micro, Small and Medium Enterprises (MSMEs)

Under the Scheme, three National Awards each were given to Micro enterprises, Small enterprises and medium enterprises. For the Service Sector also, three National Awards were given to SMEs. Special Awards to Outstanding Women Entrepreneur, SC/ST entrepreneur and Entrepreneur from NER at par with the First National Award in each category are also given.

National Award for Quality Products in Micro & Small Enterprises (MSEs)

This category includes awards for achieving outstanding quality benchmarks in certain product groups, selected every year. One National Award is given for each category for the selected products.

The National Awards for Quality Products 2012 were given to eligible entrepreneurs for 8 products: (1) Essential oil and perfumery products (2) Bio-Technology Products (3) Hand Tools (4) Builders Hardware (5) Electrical Home Appliances (6) Electro- Medical Instruments/ Equipments (7) Glass Tableware Products (8) Bakery Products.

National Awards for Lean Manufacturing Techniques

The National Award for Lean Manufacturing Techniques has been introduced this year which included three awards one each in Micro, Small and Medium enterprises categories.

National Awards to Banks for Excellence in MSE Lending and Excellence in Lending to Micro Enterprises

With a view to encourage the Banks for taking effective steps for enhancing flow of credit to the MSE sector, a National Award is conferred upon the Banks in recognition of their outstanding performance in financing the Micro and Small enterprises. Further, the National Awards for Excellence in lending to Micro enterprises have also been instituted from 2005-06.

8. Financial Assistance to MSME Industries

A net-work of Stat Financial Corporations, National Small Industries Corporation, State Small Industries Corporations, Commercial Banks, Cooperative Banks, and Regional Rural Banks provides financial assistance to MSME units. Small Industries Development Bank of India provides re-finance to the industrial loans advanced by these institutions to the MSME sector.

9. Export Promotion

Trade exhibitions are held abroad and export worthy MSME units are given opportunity and assistance in exhibiting their selected items in these exhibitions. SIDO provides assistance towards handling, clearing, insurance, publicity, freight etc., without recovering this expenditure from the participants. The trade enquires generated in these exhibitions are circulated. The trade delegations and sales-cum-study teams are sponsored from the small scale sector under the MDA Scheme of the Ministry of Commerce which provides reimbursement of 60% of the expenditure. In addition to participation in external exhibitions, these organizations also participate in various exhibitions in collaboration with other concerned organizations.

The import-Export Policy allows various exports/imports entitlements to exporting units under various schemes covered under the policy. These schemes primarily relate to advance licensing scheme, imports under Indo-US MOU, scheme of 100% EOUs, and setting up of units in FTZs/EPZs. The proposals received from SSI units are considered and recommended for granting of various licenses entitlements to the importers to help them to meet their requirements of materials etc. Imports under some of the schemes are allowed without payment of customs duty. The current import policy has, for the first time, allowed import licenses to the service centres approved by this organization for import of spares for Rs.1 lakes per annum. The cases for such imports are scrutinised for recommending the needed imports. The Export- Import policy provides for double weight age on exports from small scale units for recognition as Export /Trading Houses.

CHAPTER-IV

INDUSTRIAL POLICIES AND LEGAL FRAME WORK FOR MSMEs

4.1. Introduction

In India, MSMEs have been given an important place for both ideological and economic reasons. It is well documented that the MSMEs' industries have an important role in the development of the country. It contributes almost 40% of the gross industrial value added in the Indian economy. Government's approach and intention towards industries in general and MSMEs in particular are revealed in Industrial policy Resolutions. There are many Government Policies for development and promotion of MSMEs Industries in India. These are mentioned as below:

1. Industrial Policy Resolution (IPR) 1948.
2. Industrial Policy Resolution (IPR) 1956.
3. Industrial Policy Resolution (IPR) 1977.
4. Industrial Policy Resolution (IPR) 1980.
5. Industrial Policy Resolution (IPR) 1990&1991.
6. Comprehensive Policy Package for small scale and tiny sector, 2000-01.
7. Industrial Policy Packages for small scale industries, 2001-02.
8. Policy Package for small and medium enterprises, 2005-06.
9. Enactment of Micro, Small and Medium Enterprises Development Act, 2006.
10. North east industrial and investment promotion policy (NEIIPP), 2007.

4.2. Industrial Policy Resolution (IPR) 1948

The IPR, 1948 acknowledged the importance of small-scale industries in the overall industrial development of the country. It was well understood that small-scale industries are mainly suited for the utilization of local resources and for creation of employment opportunities. However, they have to face severe problems of raw materials, capital, skilled labour, marketing since a long period of time Therefore; government put more emphasis on the IPR, 1948 so that these problems of small-scale enterprises should be solved by the Central Government with the cooperation of the State Governments. It can be established that the main drive of IPR 1948, as far as small-scale enterprises were concerned, was 'safeguard'. The IPR of 1948 indicated that "Cottage and small scale industries have a very important role in the national economy. Offering as they do scope for individual, village or cooperative enterprise, and means for the rehabilitation of displaced persons.

These industries are particularly suited for the better utilization of local resources and for the achievement of the local self-sufficiency in respect of certain types of essential consumer goods like food, cloth and agricultural implements" (Industrial Policy Resolution, 1948).

The IPR of 1948 revealed the emergence of a dualistic approach in government policy i.e. emphasis on both traditional and modern small scale sector. This approach has continued to form the basis of industrial policy towards the small scale sector ever since. The industrial Development and Regulation Act, 1951 which was transmitted in order to provide the organizational support to IPR of 1948 provide scope for a synchronized development of cottage and small scale industries within the general framework of large scale development programmes.

4.3. Industrial Policy Resolution (IPR) 1956

This policy was first comprehensive statement on industrial development of India. The 1956 policy continued to constitute the basic economic policy for a long time. This fact has been confirmed in all the Five-Year Plans of India According to this Resolution, the objective of the social and economic policy in India was the establishment of a socialistic pattern of civilization. It provided more powers to the governmental mechanism. It laid down three categories of industries which are mentioned below:

- Schedule A: Those industries which were to be an exclusive responsibility of the state.
- Schedule B: Those which were to be progressively state-owned and in which the state would generally set up new enterprises, but in which private enterprise would be expected only to supplement the effort of the state.
- Schedule C: All the remaining industries and their future development would, in general be left to the initiative and enterprise of the private sector.

The main contribution of the IPR 1948 was that it set in the nature and pattern of industrial development in the country. The post-IPR 1948 period was marked by substantial developments taken place in the country. For example, planning has proceeded on an organized manner and the First Five Year Plan 1951-56 had been completed. Industries (Development and Regulation) Act, 1951 was also announced to legalize and control industries in the country. The parliament had also acknowledged 'the socialist pattern of society' as the basic objective of social and economic policy during this period. It was this background that the declaration of a new industrial policy resolution appeared essential. This came in the form of IPR 1956.

The IPR has aim to guarantee that decentralized sector acquires sufficient vitality to self-supporting and its development is incorporated with that of large-scale industry in the country.

Besides, the Small-Scale Industries Board (SSIB) established a working group in 1959 to scrutinize and formulate a development plan for small-scale industries during the, Third Five Year Plan, 1961-66. In the Third Five Year Plan period, specific developmental projects like 'Rural Industries Projects' and 'Industrial Estates Projects' were started to support the small-scale sector in the nation. The IPR 1956 for small-scale industries intended at 'Protection plus Development.' In a way, the IPR 1956 started the modern SSI in India. It was documented that in 1955, Planning Commission setup a Committee on village and small scale industries. The Committee suggested some important measures like:

- Reservation of certain items only for village and small scale industries.
- Restriction of capacity expansion of large industry.
- Management of supply of raw materials.
- A scheme of concessions and benefits to small producers.

The IPR of 1956 advocated the policy of protection as endorsed by this Committee to improve economic feasibility and competitive power of small scale industries. This policy stated that The State has been following a policy of supporting cottage and village and small scale industries by restricting the volume of production in the large scale sector by differential taxation or by direct subsidies. While such measures will continue to be taken, whenever necessary, the aim of the State Policy is to ensure that the decentralized sector acquires sufficient vitality to be self-supporting and its development is integrated with that of large-scale industry. The State, therefore, concentrates on measures designed to improve the competitive strength of the small scale producer. For this it is essential that the technique of production should be constantly improved and the pace of transformation being regulated so as to avoid as far as possible, technological unemployment. Lack of technical and financial assistance, of suitable working accommodation and inadequacy of facilities for repair and maintenance are among the serious handicaps of small scale producers. A start has been made with the establishment of industrial estates and rural community workshops to make good to these deficiencies. The extension of rural electrification, and the availability of power at prices, which the workers can afford, will also be of considerable help. Many of the activities relating to small scale production will be greatly helped by the organization of industrial cooperatives.

Such cooperatives should be encouraged in every way and the State should give constant attention to the development of cottage and village and small scale industry" (Industrial Policy Resolution, 1956). Main emphasis of this policy is to support to cottage, village and small industries by differential taxation or direct grants in the form of financial assistance to improve and modernize the techniques of production and competitive strength of SSIs.

4.4. Industrial Policy Resolution (IPR) 1977

This policy was announced by Janata Dal in 1977. During the two decades after the IPR 1956, the economy countersigned uneven industrial development skewed in favour of large and medium sector, on the one hand, and increase in joblessness, on the other. This situation led to a transformed emphasis on industrial policy. This gave advent to IPR 1977. This policy supported the development of small scale and cottage industries as a remedy to common problem of unemployment and regional dissimilarities in industrial development this policy proclaimed that "The main thrust of the new Industrial Policy will be on effective promotion of cottage and small industries widely dispersed in rural areas and small towns. It is the policy of the Government that whatever can be produced by small and cottage industries must only be so produced" (Industrial Policy Resolution, 1977).

The important attributes of the IPR were:

1. 504 items were reserved for exclusive production in the small-scale industries.
2. The concept of District Industries Centre (DICs) was introduced so that in each district a single agency could meet all the requirements of SSIs under one roof.
3. Technological up gradation was emphasized in traditional sector.
4. Special marketing arrangements through the provision of services, such as, product standardization, quality control, market survey, were laid down.

The IPR 1977 grouped small sector into three broad categories:

- Cottage and Household Industries which provide self-employment on a large scale.
- Tiny sector incorporating investment in industrial units in plant and machinery up to Rs.1 lakh and situated in towns with a population of less than 50,000 according to 1971 Census.
- Small-scale industries comprising of industrial units with an investment of up to Rs.10 lakhs and in case of ancillary units with an investment up to Rs.15 lakhs.

The measures suggested for the promotion of small-scale and cottage industries included:

i. Reservation of 504 items for exclusive production in small-scale sector.

ii. Proposal to set up in each district an agency called "District Industry Centre" (DIC) to serve as a focal point of development for small-scale and cottage industries. The scheme of DIC was introduced in May 1978. The main goal of setting up DICs was to promote under a single roof all the services and support required by small and village businesspersons.

4.5. Industrial Policy Resolution (IPR) 1980

The Industrial Policy of 1980 marked a major breakthrough in the policy of development of small scale industries in India. The Government of India accepted a new Industrial Policy Resolution (IPR) on July 23, 1980. The IPR wanted to synchronise the development in small scale industries with the large and medium scale industries. Industrially backward districts were identified for faster growth of existing network of SSIs. The main purpose of IPR 1980 was defined as assisting an increase in industrial production through optimum utilization of installed capacity and expansion of industries. This policy statement focused on the need for promoting competition in domestic market, technological up gradation and modernization

The Important Measures of IPR-1980

1. Increase in investment ceilings from Rs.1 lakh to Rs.2 lakhs in case of tiny units, from Rs.10 lakhs to Rs.20 lakhs in case of small-scale units and from Rs.15 lakhs to Rs.25 lakhs in case of ancillaries.

2. Introduction of the concept of nucleus plants to replace the earlier scheme of the District Industry Centres in each industrially backward district to promote the maximum small-scale industries there.

3. Promotion of village and rural industries to generate economic feasibility in the villages well compatible with the environment

4. Reservation of items and marketing support for small industries was to continue.

5. Availability of credit to growing SSI units was continued.

6. Buffer stocks of critical inputs were to continue.

7. Agricultural base was to strengthen by providing preferential treatment to agro based industries.

8. An early warning system was to establish to avoid sickness and take appropriate remedial measures.

Thus, the IPR 1980 reemphasised the spirit of the IPR 1956. The small-scale sector still continued the best sector to create employment and self-employment based opportunities in the country.

4.6.   Industrial Policy Resolution (IPR) 1990

IPR 1990 was declared during June 1990. As to the small-scale sector, the resolution continued to give significance to small-scale enterprises to serve the objective of employment generation. This policy emphasized on the need of modernization and technology up gradation to meet the objectives of employment generation and dispersal of industry in rural areas, and to enhance the contribution of small scale industries to exports.

The Important Measures of IPR-1990

- The investment ceiling in plant and machinery for small-scale industries (fixed in 1985) was raised from Rs.35 lakhs to Rs.60 lakhs and correspondingly, for ancillary units from Rs.45 lakhs to Rs.75 lakhs.
- Investment ceiling for small units had been increased from Rs.2 lakhs to Rs.5 lakhs provided the unit is located in an area having a population of 50,000 as per 1981 Census.
- As many as 836 items were reserved for exclusive manufacture in small- scale sector.
- A new scheme of Central Investment Subsidy entirely for small-scale sector in rural and backward areas capable of generating more employment at lower cost of capital had been mooted and implemented.
- In order to improve the competitiveness of the products manufactured in the small-scale sector; programmes of technology up gradation will be executed under the umbrella of an apex Technology Development Centre in Small Industries Development Organization (SIDO).
- To guarantee both satisfactory and timely flow of credit services for the small- scale industries, a new apex bank known as "Small Industries Development Bank of India (SIDBI)" was established in 1990.
- There is more emphasis on training of women and youth under Entrepreneurship Development Programme (EDP) and to establish a special cell in SIDO for this purpose.

4.7.   Industrial Policy Resolution of 1991

In the year of 1991, the Government lunched "Structural Adjustment Programme" which has resulted in radical change in the policies governing the different facets of Indian economy. In order to impart more vitality and growth to small scale sector, the Government of India declared a separate policy statement for small, tiny and village enterprises. The basic drive of this resolution was to make simpler regulations and procedures by de-licensing, deregulating, and decontrolling.

Important features of this policy are under:

- SSIs were exempted from licensing for all articles of manufacture.
- The investment limit for tiny enterprises was raised to Rs.5 lakh irrespective of location.
- Equity participation by other industrial undertakings was permitted up to a limit of 24 percent of shareholding in SSIs.
- Factoring services were to launch to solve the problem of delayed payments to SSIs.
- Priority was accorded to small and tiny units in allocation of indigenous and raw materials.
- Market promotion of products was highlighted through co-operatives, public institutions and other marketing agencies and corporations.
  Basically, the Industrial Policy Resolution of 1991 delineated developmental, deregulatory and de-bureaucratic measures and underscored the need to shift from subsidized and cheap credit to a system which would ensure acceptable flow of credit on timely and normative basis to the small scale industrial sector.

4.8.   Comprehensive Policy Package for Small Scale and Tiny Sector, 2000-01

This policy was declared by the Government of India for the development and promotion of small scale and tiny sector which has major objective to increase the competitiveness of the sector.

Important Features of IPR-2000-01:

- The exemption for excise duty limit raised from Rs.50 lakh to Rs.1 crore.
- The limit of investment was increased in industry related service and business enterprises from Rs.5 lakh to Rs.10 lakh.

- The coverage of ongoing Integrated Infrastructure Development (IID) was enhanced to cover all areas in the country with 50 percent reservation for rural areas and 50 percent earmarking of plots for tiny sector.
- The family income eligibility limit of Rs.24000 was enhanced to Rs.40000 per annum under the Prime Minister Rozgar Yojana (PMRY).
- The scheme of granting Rs.75000 to each small scale enterprise for obtaining ISO 9000 certification was continued till the end of 10th plan.

4.9. Industrial Policy Packages for small scale industries, 2001-02

- The investment limit was enhanced from Rs.1 crore to Rs.5 crore for units in hosiery and hand tool sub sectors.
- The corpus fund set up under the Credit Guarantee Fund Scheme was increased from Rs.125 crore to Rs.200 crore.
- Credit Guarantee cover was provided against an aggregate credit of Rs.23 crore till December 2001.
- Fourteen items were de-reserved in June 2001 related to leather goods, shoes and toys.
- Market Development Assistant Scheme was launched exclusively for SSI sector. VI. Four UNIDO assisted projects were commissioned during the year under the Cluster Development Programme.

4.10. Policy Package for Small and Medium Enterprises, 2005-06

In 2005-06, the Government declared a policy package for small and medium enterprises. The main attributes of this policy package were:

- The Ministry of Small Scale Industries has identified 180 items for de-reservation.
- Small and Medium Enterprises were recognized in the services sector, and were treated at par with SSIs in the manufacturing sector.
- Insurance cover was extended to approximately 30,000 borrowers, identified as chief promoters in the small scale sector.
- Emphasis was placed on Cluster Development model not only to promote manufacturing but also to renew industrial towns and build new industrial townships.

The model is currently being implemented, in nine sectors including khadi and village industries, handlooms, handicrafts, textiles, agricultural products and medicinal plants.

4.11. Enactment of Micro, Small and Medium Enterprises Development Act, 2006

In May' 2006, the President has modified the Government of India (Allocation of Business) Rules, 1961; Ministry of Agro and Rural Industries and Ministry of Small Scale Industries have been merged into a single Ministry, namely, "Ministry of Micro, Small and Medium Enterprises. As a result, the Micro, Small and Medium enterprises Development (MSMED) Act was endorsed, which offers the first ever legal framework for recognition of the concept 'enterprises' against 'industries' and integrating the three tiers of these enterprises viz. micro, small and medium and clearly fixed the investment limits for both manufacturing and service enterprises. It also provides for a statutory consultative tool at the national level with wide representation of all sections of stakeholders, particularly the three classes of enterprises.

4.12. North East Industrial and Investment Promotion Policy (NEIIPP), 2007

Due to backwardness of the North Eastern region, the Government of India broadcasted a new industrial policy for the NER including Sikkim. The policy termed as 'North East Industrial and Investment Promotion Policy (NEIIPP), 2007'. Its major objective is to encourage investment in the industrial sector by announcing fiscal and other incentives for the purpose of overall economic growth of this region. The policy with its package of incentives is intended to encourage development of industries so that the region overcomes its continuous backwardness. To summarize, Small scale and cottage industrial sector has developed rapidly in several developing and industrialised economies of the world. In India, they have emerged as a dynamic sector of Indian economy through their important contribution to GDP, industrial production and export. The advancement of small scale industries has been one of the major objectives of economic planning in India. The policies have undergone change from time to time. The six Industrial Policy Resolutions and eleven Five Year Plans sustained a continuous flow of incentives, both protective and promotional in nature, as an element of development strategy to meet socioeconomic objectives such as employment generation, removal of poverty and regional disparities, and optimum utilization of local resources.

CHAPTER-V

FINANCING THE MICRO, SMALL AND MEDIUM SCALE ENTERPRISES

5.1. Introduction

Finance holds the key to industrial development and it is the life blood of the economy. All the industries, big, medium or small require capital. The Government of India as part of its policy for promotion of the small scale sector has set up a number of institutions to meet the financing requirements of this sector.

5.2. Types of Loans

The requirements of finance can be broadly classified into three categories, viz., according to the duration of the credit required.

1. Short-term Finance or working capital finance which is required for day-to-day operations of the enterprise and it is provided in the form of cash credit, over draft facility and bills purchase and discount facility. Short-term credit is also required for stocking raw materials, parts components, and sub assemblies required for producing /assembly of the end product.

2. Medium-term finance which is needed for small tools, implements and minor repairs etc.

3. Long-term finance needed for buying machinery and equipments or for the provision of land, factory building and other fixed assets. Medium and long-term credit (also known as term finance) is required both at the time of starting an enterprise and expansion of its productive capacity by replacing or adding the existing equipment.

The term "finance" sanctioned in the form of "term loan " is required for:

i)   Land and site development.

ii) Building and civil works

iii) Plant and Machinery

iv) Installation expenses and,

v)   Miscellaneous fixed assets which comprises vehicles, furniture and fixtures, Office equipment, workshop and laboratory equipment, miscellaneous tools including erection tools, equipment for distribution of water & power supply and treatment of water, fire fighting equipments, affluent treatment etc.

Another element of miscellaneous fixed cost, particularly, in respect of units to be located in backward areas is the expenditure on infrastructure facilities like water supply, power connection, roads, transportation, etc.

5.2.1. *The Short-term Loans or Working Capital is Required for the Following*

a) Purchase of raw materials, chemicals, components, parts, sub-assemblies.

b) Consumable utilities, power, water and fuel.

c) Labour and managerial service facilities, wages, salaries, bonus, provision of provident funds etc.

d) Repairs and maintenance, light, rent and tax on factory assets, insurance of factory assets, miscellaneous factory expenses, contingency, distribution costs, financial expenditure including interest on loan, both for ling and short-term, guarantee commissions, depreciation etc. working capital facilities as are available from the commercial banks may be classified as :

    i.   Dock and key pledge of stocks

    ii.   Factory/mundy type hypothecation advances (pending statement of stocks held by the Unit to be intimated to the banks)

    iii.   Advance against stock in process

    iv.   Advance against bills(when finished goods are supplied on credit)

    v.   Clean advance (contingency needs)

    vi.   Packing credit to exporters for executing export orders.

It is advisable that the working capital is never allowed to be inadequate which calls for on the one hand saving the unit from trading and on the other arranging for necessary stocks and requirements to be pledged as per arrangement with the bank. Otherwise, the inadequate working capital can result in the following;

i) Hampers the growth of the enterprise because it becomes difficult for the entrepreneur to undertake profitable projects on account of non-availability of working capital funds.

ii) It becomes difficult to implement operating plans and achieve the targeted profits.

iii) Operating inefficiencies creep in, when it becomes difficult even to meet day-to-day commitments.

iv) Sometimes the paucity of the working capital renders the enterprise unable to avail of attractive credit.

v) Fixed assets cannot be put to optimum use which affects the rate of investment.

Working capital finance is sanctioned in the form of cash credit, overdraft facility and bills purchased coupled with discounting facility. Working capital is an investment in the current assets. In any industrial enterprise, initially cash is converted into raw materials which are converted into work in process and into financial goods and back to cash. These processes are being continuous results into blocking of some of the amount in this cycle. The working capital or the level of investment in the operating cycle depends on:

a) Changes in the terms of production, sales, while other factors are constant.

b) Change in the price of raw material, time required to produce these, changes in the manufacturing techniques, process of manufacture, policy etc.

5.3.   Financial Institutions

Since the second five year plan (1956-61) several institutions have been created to provide financial assistance to small scale units on a preferential basis. For granting credit facilities, small scale industrial units are treated as one of the priority sectors by commercial banks and other financial agencies. The total credit extended by scheduled commercial banks to small scale units as on December 1978 amounted to Rs.2,766 crores as against Rs.286 crores as on June 30, 1969. The extent of credit increased to Rs.3,299 crores in 1981; Rs.6,612 crores in 1985 and Rs.7,808 crores in 1986. The Asian Development Bank (ADB) is also extending its help in financing industrial estate project and promoting development of ancillary industrial units. The International Development Association (IDA), an officiate of the world Bank had sanctioned a line of credit for 25 million dollars to the government of India, the rupee equivalent of which is available to the Industrial Development Bank of India for refinancing loans given by state financial corporations to small and medium-sized industrial units for financing imports of equipments and of technical know-how from abroad. Generally, small units find it difficult to have access to various institutional agencies supplying finance mainly because of the lack of adequate security. In order to overcome this difficulty, the Reserve Bank of India evolved the credit guarantee scheme in 1960 for guarantee of advance granted to small-scale units. Under the credit guarantee scheme, credit institutions were required to pay to the guarantee organisation, a guarantee commission at the rate of one fourth per cent per annum on the amount of guarantee issued. As a result of these incentives, there has been a considerable improvement in the financing of small-scale industries by credit institutions. In this Connection, the last ten years Credit outstanding from MSMEs is exhibited in the following Table 4.1.

Table 4.1: Outstanding Bank Credit to Micro and Small Enterprises

(Rs. Crore)

As on last reporting Friday of March	Public Sector Banks	Private Sector Banks	Foreign Banks	All Scheduled Commercial Banks
2005	67,800	8,592	6,907	83,498
2006	82,434 (21.6)	10,421 (21.3)	8,430 (22.1)	1,01,285 (21.3)
2007	1,02,550 (24.4)	13,136 (26.1)	11,637(38.0)	1,27,323 (25.7)
2008	1,51,137 (47.4)	46,912 (257.1)	15,489 (33.1)	2,13,538 (67.7)
2009	1,91,408 (26.6)	46,656 (0.0)	18,063 (16.6)	2,56,127 (19.9)
2010	2,78,398 (45.4)	64,534 (38.3)	21,069 (16.6)	3,64,012# (42.1)
2011 Provisional	3,76,625 (35.3)	87,857 (36.1)	21,461 (1.9)	4,85,943 (33.5)
2012	3,96,343 (5.24)	1,10,514(25.79)	(21,760)(1.05)	(5,28,617) (8.77)
2013	5,02,459(26.71)	154732 (40.01)	30020(37.95)	687209(30.00)
2014	615976(22.59)	200138(29.35)	30020(0.01)	864135(23.13)

Source: MSME Annual Report 2014-15, Government of India, Pp-245

Financial institutions rendering promotional assistance and credit facilities assistance to small scale industries are:

a) Commercial Banks

All Commercial Banks

b) All India Lending Institutions

1. Industrial development Bank of India (IDBI) Small Industries Development Bank of India (SIDBI). Various schemes of the IDBI/SIDBI are:
   a) Refinance Schemes for industrial loans
   b) Special schemes for assistance to artisans and village and cottage industries, scheduled tribes/scheduled caste entrepreneurs, physically handicapped entrepreneurs and small scale industrial units,
   c) Refinance scheme for rehabilitation of small enterprises
   d) Refinance scheme for modernization of small industries
   e) Seed capital scheme
   f) Bills rediscounting scheme
   g) Assistance through National Small industries Corporation
   h) Scheme to assist women entrepreneurs etc.
2. Industrial Finance Corporation for India (IFCI)
3. Industrial Credit and Investment Corporation of India (ICICI)

4. Industrial Reconstruction Bank of India (IRBI)

5. Export Import Bank of India (EXIM Bank)

6. National Bank for Agriculture & Rural Development (NABARD)

7. National Cooperative Development Corporation (NCDC)

C) Other Financial Institutions

1. State Financial Corporations(SFCs)

2. Export Credit Guarantee Corporation (ECGC)

3. Deposit Insurance and Credit Guarantee Corporation (DICGC)

4. Regional Rural Bank and Cooperative Banks

5. National Small Industries Corporation (NSIC)

6. State Small Industries Corporation.

5.4.   Role of Banks

Credit is an essential input for any industrial enterprise. Small Scale Industrial units, almost everywhere in the world, face the problem of non-availability of adequate credit facilities both in respect of working capital and medium and long-term funds.

Government of India having recognized the importance of small scale industries in the overall industrial development as also overall economic development of the country, has been engaged in formulating suitable policies and active programmes from time to time with a view to assisting small scale units in meeting their credit requirements.

After nationalization of the major Indian commercial banks as also recognition of small scale industries as one of the priority sectors of material economy. Performance of the banking sectors in this regard has been improving progressively.

5.4.1. Reserve Bank of India

The Reserve Bank of India was established on April 1, 1935 in accordance with the provisions of the Reserve Bank of India Act., 1934 and was nationalized in 1948. As the apex bank in the country, the Reserve Bank of India (RBI) lays down the policies of lending, supervision and follows up of advance to small scale industrial units which are recognized as priority sector.

The main functions of Reserve Bank of India are note issuing, acting as banker's bank and banker to government etc. An important function of the Reserve Bank of India is regulation of credit and banking system in the country. The RBI has the power to influence or initiate, to expand or contract the volume of credit either by direct or indirect methods. For this, the Reserve Bank is armed with many powers to control the money market of India. By changing the Bank rate, by increasing the ratio of reserves of the scheduled banks and by open market operations, it may try to influence the volume of credit in the country.

Reserve Bank of India introduced "service Area approach" with the idea of making banks to devote their energy and resources to develop their adjoining area; therefore, each branch was entrusted with the responsibility of providing finance to accelerate the growth process in the local areas.

In a view of the fact that the small scale enterprises have a week capital base and they often find it difficult to offer acceptable securities, the Reserve Bank of India evolved a new scheme in 1960 known as "credit guarantee scheme" for guarantee of advances granted to small scale units by institutional agencies. Under this scheme, the guarantee organization stands surety on behalf of the small scale units and guarantees loans granted to them up to a certain limit against default or bad debt. The idea behind the introduction of this scheme is that the banks and other lending institutions should have assurance of security while dealing with the small scale industrial sector. Under this scheme, credit institutions were required to pay to the guarantee organization, a guarantee commission at the rate of one fourth (1/4) per cent per annum o the amount of guarantee issued. Initially the scheme was applicable to 22 districts but, later on, it was extended to the entire country, and, at present large number of financial institutions is taking advantage of the same and are being offered guarantee cover. The scheme is being reviewed by the RBI from time to time and all efforts are made to make the scheme to the best advantage of the small scale industrial units..

A notable step taken in the financing of the small scale industries by the Reserve Bank of India (RBI) is introduction of the "Lead Bank" scheme under which each district, in the country has been allotted to one of the major Indian Banks for intensive development of banking facilities.

5.4.2. *Commercial Banks*

Commercial Banks in India comprises the State Bank of India (SBI) and its subsidiaries, nationalized banks, foreign banks and other scheduled commercial banks, regional rural banks and non- scheduled commercial banks. The total number of branched of commercial banks are more than 45000 and the regional rural banks are approximately 8000 covering 280 districts in the country. Commercial banks mostly provide short term and in some cases medium term financial assistance also to small scale units. According to the Data compiled by RBI, of all the advances given to small scale industries by the commercial banks, the share of 'term loan' is nearly 30%. The lead in this regard was taken by the State Bank of India (SBI) in 1956 when a pilot scheme for guaranteed credit to small scale units was started. Initially, the scheme was confined to the branches of the SBI in the country. Subsequently, some of the other commercial banks also instalment credit for acquiring fixed assets for the purpose of establishment and extension of their units, and, term credit for meeting their working capital needs. The borrower is required to make a down payment of 20 to 33.1/3% of cost of equipment to be purchased from one's own resources while the rest is financed out of the loan. The rate of interest charged on these loans varies from time to time as per the directive of the Reserve Bank of India (RBI). The period for which this loan is granted varies from 7 to 10 years. These loans are repayable in half yearly or yearly instalments.

Most of the commercial banks have got specialized units in their administrative structure to take care of the financial needs of the small scale industrial units. The fixed capital needs or the long and medium term needs of the small scale industrial units are presently being taken care of by the banks under their integrated scheme of credit for the advances financed to meet their medium and long-term credit needs for replacement of machinery, addition of the machinery, modernisation etc. The rate of interest charged normally from the small scale industrial units is between 12% and 15% against 18% from the large scale units.

The commercial banks also establish letter of credit on behalf of their clients for favouring supplies of raw materials/machinery (both India and foreign) which extend the bankers assurance for payment and thus help their delivery. Certain transactions, particularly those in contracts of sale to government departments, may require guarantees being issued in lieu of security/earnest money deposits for release of advance money, supply of raw materials for processing, full payment of bills on assurance of performance, etc. Commercial banks issue such guarantee also.

5.5. Role of Financial Institutions

Various organizations including National Small Industries Corporation, State Smell Industries Corporation, State Financial Corporation and Commercial banks provide financial assistance to small scale units. Long term and medium term loans are available from these organizations. The Small Industries Development Bank of India provides re-finance facilities to the industrial loans advanced by these institutions to the small scale sector.

5.5.1. *Small Industries Development Bank of India (SIDBI)*

In response to the long standing demand of small scale sector in India, Small Industries Development Bank of India (SIDBI) was set up, by an Act of parliament, as an apex institution for promotion, financing and development of industries in the small scale sector and for co-ordinating the functions of other institutions engaged in similar activities. SIDBI, was set up as a wholly owned subsidiary of Industrial Development Bank of India (IDBI), commenced its operations during 1990 with its head office at Lucknow and a network of 5 regional offices and 21 branch offices throughout the country. Small Industries Development Bank of India (SIDBI) under its charted, has been, inter alia, assigned the task of being the main purveyor of term finance to the small scale sector in the country. Small scale industrial units, artisans, village and cottage industrial units in the tiny sector and small road transport operators are extended financial assistance mainly by way of refinance through primary lending institutions (PLIs) viz. State Financial Corporations (SFCs), State Industrial Development Corporation/state Industrial Investment Corporations (SIDCs/SIICs) and banks which have a wide network of branches. Term loans extended by eligible PLIs to small industrial projects, irrespective of the location and form of organization of the units, are eligible for refinance assistance. The activities of SIDBI are as under:

(a) Refinancing of loans and advances extended by the primary lending institutions to industrial concerns in the small scale sector and also providing resource support to them.

(b) Discounting and rediscounting of bills arising from sale of machinery to, or manufactured by, industrial concerns in the small scale sector.

(c) Extension of seed capital/soft loan assistance under National Equity Fun, Mahila Udayam Nidhi and seed Capital Schemes through specified lending agencies.

(d) Granting direct assistance as well as refinancing of loans extended by primary lending institutions for financing export of products manufactured by industrial concerns in the small scale sector.

(e) Providing services like factoring, leasing etc. to industrial concerns in the small sector.

(f) Extending financial support to National Small Industries Corporation for providing leasing, hire-purchase and marketing support to SSI units.

The immediate thrust of SIDBI is on:

(i) initiating steps for technological up gradation and modernization of existing units;

(ii) expanding the channels for marketing the products of SSI sector in domestic and overseas markets;

(iii) Promotion of employment oriented industries especially in semi- urban areas to create more employment opportunities and thereby checking migration of population to urban and cosmopolitan areas.

Eligibility for Refinance

Term-loans extended by eligible institutions to small scale industrial projects irrespective of the location and form of organization of the unit are eligible for refinance assistance.

SIDBI provides refinance at concessional rate of interest in respect of loans to certain special category of borrowers.

Presently, the institutions eligible for availing of refinance facilities from SIDBI comprise 18 state financial corporation's(SFCs), 26 state Industrial Development Corporations/State Industrial Investment corporations, 76 Commercial Banks, 196 Regional Rural Banks (RRBs), 11 State Co-operative Banks and 524 Central and Urban Co-operative Banks.

Procedure for availing Loan/Refinance

Intending borrowers have to approach eligible institutions. All offices of SDIBI process refinance proposals as the operations are fully decentralized, under their respective jurisdictions. The eligible institutions first sanction assistance to the borrowers and having complied with certain procedures laid down, refinance sanction and disbursals are sought by the institutions from SIDBI.

Schemes of Assistance

SIDBI offers various schemes for the development of small entrepreneurs throughout the country. Details of individual schemes are as follows:

1. General Scheme

For all forms of organizations in the small scale sector to set up new small scale units or expansion of existing units, SIDBI provides refinance for industrial loans for small and village industries under this scheme.

2. Composite Loan Scheme

The scheme covers composite loans up to Rs.50,000 sanctioned to artisans, village and cottage industries and small industries in the tiny sector by eligible institutions. Assistance is provided for equipment and/or working capital. For artisans, assistance is available irrespective of location while for others the project should be located in areas with population not exceeding 5 lakhs.

As the loans can be covered neither under the credit Guarantee Scheme of DICGC, eligible institutions have been advised nor to insist on collateral security.

3. Scheme for SC/ST & Physically Handicapped Entrepreneurs

This scheme provides assistance for equipment and/or working capital, irrespective of location.

4. Specific Schemes

For all forms of organizations in the small scale for the purpose of acquisition of

a) In-house quality control facilities
b) Pollution control equipment
c) Computers
d) For indigenization/import substitution
e) For manufacturing and renewable energy/energy saving systems etc.

The scheme has been drawn up to encourage SSI units to establish facilities for testing and quality control and other facilities with a view to ensuring better market acceptability of their products. The assistance is provided by way of term loan normally not exceeding Rs.7.5 laths per project.

5. *National Equity Fund Scheme (NEF)*

SIDBI introduced this scheme, in order to meet gap in equity and with the objective of providing equity type of support to small entrepreneurs of tiny/small scale sector and, for rehabilitation of viable sick units in the SSI sector.

Eligibility

a) Entrepreneurs setting up new projects in the tiny and small scale sector for manufacture, preservation or processing of goods and, existing sick SSI units undertaking rehabilitation, if they are found to be potentially viable by the financing institutions, are eligible for assistance.

b) All industrial activities and service industries, except road transport, hotel, restaurant and hospitals/nursing homes, are eligible for assistance under the Scheme.

c) The unit should be located in village/town having population upto 5 laths (15 laths in the case of hilly areas and North-Eastern Region). However, in the case of the rehabilitation proposals, the project could be located in towns/villages with population upto 15 laths.

d) New projects which avail for any margin money or seed/special capital assistance under the schemes of Central or State Government, SFCs and other State-level institutions or banks (except Central/State Investment Subsidy) will not be eligible for assistance.

e) The rehabilitation proposal should conform to the norms prescribed under the Rehabilitation Refinance Scheme of SDBI for SSI sector.

f) The unit should be registered with State Directorate of Industries/appropriate statutory authority.

g) The unit should be eligible for assistance under the Refinance Scheme for SIDBI. Sanction of refinance in respect of term loan for the project by SIDBI is a prerequisite for extending equity type assistance under the Scheme.

h) The total fund requirement of project in the form of equity assistance under NEF, term loan and working capital will be provided by a single agency. Central/State subsidy may be retained for meeting working capital requirement.

6. *Special Scheme for Assistance to Ex-servicemen (Including Widows of ex-servicemen)*

It is sponsored by Director General (Resettlement), ministry of defense, Government of India to set up small industrial projects including service industries and transport activity which are eligible for finance as per SSI norms.

7. *Seed Capital Scheme*

It is sanctioned for technically or professionally qualified entrepreneurs or entrepreneurs with relevant experience or skills in industry/business to meet the gap in prescribed promoter's contribution or in equity.

8. *Single Window Scheme*

Under this scheme refinance is provided for working capital loan availed by entrepreneurs from SFCs/SIDCs for setting up new projects in MSME sector.

New Micro and small scale units whose project cost does not exceed Rs.10 lakhs and the total working capital requirement at the normal level of operation is up to Rs.5 laths, provided the unit has been sanctioned term loan for fixed assets and working capital loan by the same institution are eligible for the scheme. Under this scheme, permissible term loan for fixed assets and working capital loan up to Rs.5 laths are provided. There is no commitment charge. The debt-equity ratio should be 3:1 for the total venture outlay (i.e. cost of the project plus total working capital requirements) after taking account the amount of investment subsidy/ incentive available for the project. The current assets are to be hypothecated towards security.

State financial corporation's (SFCs) and the twin-function SIDCS are the eligible financial institutions under this scheme.

9. *Scheme for Women Entrepreneurs for Setting up MSME Units. The Scheme has been Formulated with the Twin Objectives of*

a. Providing training and extension services support to women entrepreneurs and, extending financial assistance on concessional terms to enable them to set up industrial units in the small scale sector. Programmes for training and extension services for women entrepreneurs are organized through designated/approved agencies. All projects in SSI sector including cottage, village and tiny industries, promoted and managed by women entrepreneurs are eligible for concessional assistance under the scheme.

b. Mahila Udayam Nidhi (MUN) scheme for women entrepreneurs to meet gap in equity while setting up new industrial projects in the small scale sector as also for service activities which are eligible for finance as per SSI norms. The scheme is operated through SFCs/twin function SIDCs.

Under this scheme, soft loan limited up to 15% of cost of project is provided and the service charge is 1% per annum on soft loan.

10. Schemes of Incentives for Exports

Besides providing export incentives, to promote export capability of SSI units, the small Industries Development Bank of India (SIDBI) has announced the formation of the Technology Development and modernization Fund (TDMF) with an initial amount of Rs.200 crores.

The new scheme is to encourage existing units to modernise their production facilities and adopt improved and updated technology so as to strengthen their export capabilities. Units which are already exporting their products or have the potential to export at least 25% of the output by adopting modernization scheme would be eligible for assistance from the fund, provided, they have been in operation for atleast 3 years and are not the default to banks/financial institutions. Assistance under the scheme is available for:

1. Acquisition of capital equipment.
2. Cost of know-how(including designs and drawings)
3. Up gradation of process technology with thrust on quality improvement.
4. Improvement in packaging
5. Cost of total quality management (TQM) and
6. Acquisition of ISO 9000 certification.

Those seeking assistance under the scheme are required to make a minimum level of promoter's contribution of 20% of the project cost. SIDBI'S assistance would be in the form of direct term loan or contribution to equity share capital of the company or both.

Assistance will be need-based subject to a minimum of Rs.10 laths per unit. SIDBI has proposed to charge its prime lending rate for the term loan sanctioned under the scheme with no upfront fee.

11. Equipment Refinance Scheme

It is implemented for existing MSME units in operation for at least 4 years with dividend record during preceding two accounting years and not in default to institutions/banks. Refinance is provided for identifiable items of equipment machinery for diversification/ expansion/replacement and also balancing equipment/self-fabricated equipment. Second hand machineries are not eligible.

12. Refinance Scheme for Modernization of MSMEs' Industries

The primary objective of the scheme is to encourage industrial units overcome the backlog of modernization and to adopt improved and updated technology and methods of production and to prevent mechanical and technological obsolescence. Modernisation may include replacement or renovation of plant and machinery or acquisition of balancing equipment for fuller and more effective utilization of installed capacity.

13. Scheme for Small Road Transport operations

It is owing not more than six vehicles to meet expenditure towards cost of chassis, body building, initial taxes/insurance and working capital. Second hand vehicles are not eligible for assistance.

14. Bills Rediscounting Scheme

SIDBI's assistance to small scale sector flows through its scheme of rediscounting of bills/ promissory notes arising out of sales of indigenous machinery to purchaser-user on deferred payment basis on special concessional rates of discount/rediscount for purchaser-user as well as seller manufacturers in this sector. There is no minimum limit for transaction under the scheme. The facilities under the scheme are available for purchase o machinery for expansion, diversification and modernization. New SSI units can also avail of the facilities under the scheme for purchase of machinery. An advance drawn payment of 15% is usually insisted upon under the scheme with a reduced norm of 10% applicable for commercial vehicles and textile machinery.

15. Refinance Scheme for setting up Industrial Estates

This scheme is for SIDCs corporate and co-operatives & accredited NGO's approved by KVIC. This scheme is for development of industrial estates with proper infrastructural facilities exclusively for SSI units.

16. Schemes for infrastructure development.

17. Refinance scheme under ADB line of credit.

18. Foreign currency refinance scheme.

19. Refinance scheme for rehabilitation of small scale industries.

20. Schemes for marketing activities.

21. Schemes for medical profession.

22. Schemes for tourism related activities.

23. Scheme for professionals

24. Schemes for sub-contracting units.

25. Schemes for specialized marketing agencies etc.

5.5.2. *National Small Industries Corporation (NSIC)*

The National Small Industries Corporation limited, a government of India undertaking is a pioneer in promoting and supporting small scale units all over the country since 1955. The Corporation provides support to small industries in the following areas:

1. Helps small scale units in meeting the requirements of 'Term Loan' for the purchase of imported and indigenous machinery and to supply the same to the entrepreneurs on easy hire purchase terms.

   The supply of machines of hire-purchase is in a way, an offer of funds, an offer of foreign exchange facilities and a combination of both. NSIC takes upon itself the entire procedure starting from issue of an enquiry to the suppliers to delivery of machines, arranges foreign exchange, obtains import licence, opens letter of credit and looks after the customs requirements and clearance of machines.

   Applications from units registered with State Directorates of Industries or DIC, which are covered by the term "small scale industry" as defined by the government of India are eligible to avail the facilities.

   This Scheme was most popular in 1950s and 1960 because, prior to the nationalization of the major commercial banks, this was the only agency rendering this service to small scale units.

   Entrepreneurs wishing to avail this scheme have to pay earnest money varying from 15 to 30% of value of machinery in addition to a service charge varying from 2 to 5% depending on the value of machinery and the location of the unit. The full hiring value of the machine along with interest on unpaid amount and service charge is payable in 13 half-yearly installments-first installment falling due after one year of the installation of the machinery. In case of furnaces, boilers, cold storage, plants, tyre retreading, conning, electroplating etc., the loan has to be returned in 9 instalments. Certain special categories of entrepreneurs, such as technocrats, physically handicapped persons, defence personnel and those belonging to SC/ST are charged concessional rate of earnest money, interest and service charges.

2. Securing government orders for the small scale industries and marketing of small industries products based on consortia approach.

3. Export of small industries products and developing export worthiness of small scale units.

4. Enlisting competent units and facilitating their participation in Government stores purchase programme. Installment

5. Developing prototypes of machines, equipments and tools which are then passed on for commercial production.

6. Providing technical assistance and training in several technical trades.

7. Supply and distribution of indigenous and imported raw materials.

8. Setting up small scale industries in other developing countries on turnkey basis.

9. Securing co-ordination between small scale and large scale industries, so, that the former produces goods required by the latter.

10. Underwriting and guaranteeing loans from banks and other sources and,

11. Establishment of market Development centre's to :

   a) Play a catalytic role in providing exposure to the products of small scale units; assist their direct and indirect marketing.

   b) Provide permanent show room facilities and,

   c) Create consumer confidence in the products of SSIs. Prescribed application forms are available from the NSIC and its regional office/branches at the state to avail its facilities. These have to be submitted to the NSIC or its branches at the State/District level through the Deputy Director/Regional/Jt. Director of Industries or through the respective District Industries Centre. The application has to be accompanied by the latest quotation from the manufacturers or the suppliers of machinery approved by the NSIC. The NSIC pass 90% of the cost of machinery to the supplier and the balance 10% after getting certificate of satisfaction from the customer. NSIC also supplies machinery to existing profit making and financially viable small scale units (with permanent registration as an SSI unit) on easy leasing term.

5.5.3. State Financial Corporation (SFCs)

The State Financial Corporation (SFCs) which exist almost in every state and union territory of the country constitute the most important single source of long-term credit to small scale industries.

The wide disparities in the levels of industrial development in different states and the vast size of the country in early 1960s led to the felt need for supplementing the work of Industrial Finance Corporation of India, IFCI (a central government institution setup for meeting the credit and capital investment needs of large scale corporate bodies) by setting up a State Finance Corporation (SFC) in each state and union territory for granting 'term finance' and equity capital to small scale and medium scale industries which are mostly either ownership or partnership concerns. In places, where there are no SFCs, the Industrial Development Corporation operating in the states or union territories concerned, perform the functions of the SFCs. The SFCs have their regional offices, branches and field level officers.

State Financial Corporation grant term loans for the purchase of land, construction of factory premises and purchase of machinery and equipment for the setting up of new industries or for expansion of modernization of the existing ones. The loans granted by these corporations are payable in equal annual instalments spread over a period of 10 to 12 years, the first instalment falling due for payment after one or two years of the disbursement of the loan. Generally, advances are made up to 50 to 75% of the value of assets offered as security including those acquired out of loans.

The maximum amount of loan which can be sanctioned by SFC is Rs.60 laths in case of limited company of corporations or societies, while the relative limit in other cases including proprietary and partnership concern is Rs.30 laths. SFC's operate various schemes of financial assistance to SSI units. Most popular among them being 'composite loan schemes' which covers both term loan and working capital up to a maximum of Rs.50,000 under which no promoter's contribution is necessary. The 'Integrated loan scheme' enables the units to operate up to Rs.1 lakh inclusive of working capital component. Other schemes are also available for special category of entrepreneurs, women entrepreneurs etc.

SFCs generally prescribe a margin of 25% and allow an initial holiday of 2 years for the loan repayment.

The application for loans accompanied with a project report & other information prescribed by the SFCs are to be submitted to SFCs. The applications are considered for sanction on the basis of financial viability, technical feasibility and competence of the entrepreneurs as assessed by the corporation. On receipt of information about the sanction of loan, the entrepreneurs have to take steps that may be prescribed by the corporation for completing the documentation requirements, to facilitate drawback of loans/instalments according to the requirement of the unit. These would include execution of loan agreement, irrevocable power of attorney, deed of undertaking, guarantees etc., as may be required by the corporation.

5.5.4. *State Level Small Industries Corporations (SSICs)*

The State Small Industries Corporations (SSICs) exists almost in every state and union territories. They render assistance in meeting the long-term credit needs of the small scale nits, particularly, for industrial premises either in the form of self constructed buildings or sheds in the industrial estates.

SSICs also supply machinery on hire-purchase basis to small scale and ancillary industries, up to the value of Rs.60 laths and RS.75 laths respectively, inclusive of the value of machinery and equipment already installed. SSIC's supply is only indigenous machinery unlike NSIC, which supplies both imported and indigenous machinery. The payment for the machinery and equipment is made directly to the suppliers.

The hire-purchase value is generally recovered in 13 half yearly instalments and a rebate of 2% is allowed for payment of instalments on or before the due date.

5.5.5. *National Bank for Agriculture and Rural Development (NABARD)*

The National Bank for Agriculture and Rural Development was setup in July 1982 to provide re-finance assistance to state co-operative Banks, Regional Rural Banks and other approved institutions for all kinds of promotion and investment credit to small scale industries, artisans, cottage and village industries, handicraft and other allied activities.

NABARD has proposed recently to set up an autonomous organization known as District Rural Industries Corporation (DRIC) to focus attention on rural, small, and tiny industries in 20 districts in the country. It would be registered company with an investment of Rs.10 laths with entrepreneurs as shareholders. It would provide small and village industries with the required support finance, marketing organization and technology.

5.5.6. *Export-Import (EXIM) Bank of India*

Export Import Bank of India, set up for the purpose of financing, facilitating and promoting foreign trade of India, is the principal financial institution in the country for Co-ordinating the working of institutions engaged in financing exports and imports.

The bank presently focuses on export finance. It finances export of Indian machinery, manufactured goods, and consultancy and technology services on deferred payment terms. EXIM Bank finance is also available for export production stages. EXIM Bank under takes co-financing with global and regional development agencies and assists Indian exporters in their efforts to participate in such overseas projects.

EXIM Bank's advisory services provide access to Euro financing and global credit for Indian companies engaged in exports. The Bank works closely with Indian companies in designing financing packages for export oriented industries in India, overseas joint ventures and project.

Term finance is provided to Indian exporters of eligible goods and services which enable them to offer deferred credit to overseas buyers. Deferred credit can also cover Indian consultancy, technology and other services. Commercial banks participate in this programme directly. The financing programmes of EXIM Bank include:

1. Pre shipment credit
2. Term loan for Export production
3. Overseas investment finance
4. Finance for export marketing
5. Overseas buyers credit
6. Loan to commercial Banks in India etc

5.6. Financing under Self Employment Schemes to the Educated Unemployed Youth

In the successive five year plans special consideration has been given to the unemployed particularly among the educated youth. One such scheme launched in 1983-84 was to provide assistance to the educated unemployed youth to become self-employed by starting their own industrial enterprises, services and business establishments through a package of monetary assistance. Under this self-employment scheme, unemployed youth who have successfully completed their matriculation and are in the age group of 18 to 35 can take advantage of getting themselves registered with their district Industry Centres which number more than 400, all over the country.

Under this scheme, beneficiaries are entitled to a composite loan for an industrial venture, a service venture and a small business venture. The monetary aspect of the scheme is implemented through the lead bank in each district. The banks are not expected to insist on any collateral security for loan up to maximum ceiling. The loans sanctioned under this scheme are charged interest @ 10% per annum in specified backward areas and 12% per annum in other areas. Repayment of the loan is made in instalments, the first instalment falling due between 6 months and 10 months after the date of disbursement of the loan. The period of instalment is spread over 3 to 7 years depending upon the nature of venture and expected profitability. The recovery of the loan is the responsibility of the bank concerned. Local mangers of the banks are allowed sufficient flexibility in dealing with the defaulting borrowers particularly by re-scheduling the recovery period in case of bona fide defaulters. The District Industry Centres have been asked to monitor the implementation of the scheme at district level. Besides educational qualifications and the beneficiaries mentioned above, the youth belonging to a family with an annual income of Rs. 10,000/- and below are eligible to avail the scheme.

5.6.1. *Prime Minister's Rozgar Yojana (PMRY) for Self-Employment*

The continued rapid growth in population has long been exerting pressure on the country's resources, hindering development in wake. It has in its aftermath generated poverty and unemployment problems. Since independence much headway has been made to improve the economy but the poverty still persists. Liberalising measured of the industrial and trade structure has been taken up by the Government recently. However, unemployed youth are still not in a position to undertake projects involving investment. To sort it out, the Prime Minister's Rozgar Yojana is an ideal and dynamic channel for generating jobs to the millions of job seekers through self-employment.

The scheme was formally announced by the Prime Minister on 15th August, 1993 and launched on 2nd, October, 1993.

Objective

The Prime Minister's Rozgar Yojana (PMRY) has been designed to set up 7 lakh micro enterprises by the educated unemployed youth. It relates to the setting up of the self-employment ventures through industry, services and business routes.

Eligibility

The scheme intends to cover whole of the country. Any unemployed educated person living any part of the country rural or urban, fulfilling the following conditions will be eligible for assistance:

(i)   Age: Between 18 and 35 years.

(ii) Qualification: Metric(Passed or Failed) or ITI Passed or having undergone Government sponsored technical course for a minimum duration of 6 months.

(iii) Residency: Permanent resident of the area for at least 3 years.

(iv) Family Income: Upto Rs.24,000 per annum.

They should not be defaulters to any nationalized bank/financial institution/co-operative bank. Preference is given to weaker sections including women. The scheme envisages 22.5 per cent reservation for SC/ST and 27 percent for other backward classes (OBCs).

Project Cost

Project up to Rs.1 lakh are covered under the scheme in case of individuals. If two or more eligible persons join together in a partnership, the project with higher costs would also be covered provided share of each person in the project cost is Rs. 1 lakh or less.

Entrepreneur is required to contribute 5 per cent of project cost as margin money in cash. Balance 85 per cent would be sanctioned as composite loan by bank at the rates of interest applicable to such loans under guidelines of Reserve Bank of India (RBI) issued from time to time.

The loans would not require any collateral guarantee. Only assets created under the scheme would by hypothecated/mortgaged/pledged to the bank advancing the loan.

Subsidy

Government of India would provide subsidy at the rate of 15 percent of the project cost subject to ceiling of Rs. 7,500 per entrepreneur. In case more than one entrepreneur join together and set up a project under partnership, subsidy would be calculated for each partner separately at the rate of 15 percent of his share in the project cost, limited to Rs.7,500 (per partner).

Repayment Schedule

Repayment schedule ranges from 3 to 7 years after an initial moratorium of 6 to 18 months as decided by the bank.

5.7.   Factoring Service

Factoring is a new financial service introduced in India. It is, in fact, not just a single service, rather a portfolio of complementary financial services.

Clients (i.e., Sellers) can avail themselves of some or all of these, according to their individual needs.

The basic components of factoring services are:

- Finance up to 80% of the invoice value.
- Sales ledger administration.
- Debt collection services and
- Credit insurance.

Working Procedures of Factoring

In factoring, clients enter into a factoring arrangement with the factor, who takes responsibility for dealing with ass their receivables. Factor fixes up a limit for purchase of debts in lieu of bills discounting or other borrowing facilities against receivables from their bank, and allows prepayment up to 80% of the invoice value. The original invoice and title documents can be directly sent by clients to their customers (i.e. buyers), and only copies are handed over to the factor.

Depending upon the individual customer limits fixed by the factor, the invoices are purchased and prepayment made. The invoice carries a notice to the customer to pay the factor directly. The factor now tries to follow-up for payment. No doubt, clients assistance any be sought by the factor, but only when there are problems or disputes. It is as simple as that.

In "Recourse factoring", ultimate "Customer risk" is borne by the client, and in "Full factoring", by the factor.

Benefits of Factoring to Clients

A healthy cash flow is essential for meeting the commitments statutory or otherwise and to keep up production schedules. These days, where most of the sales are on credit, none can be sure of prompt payments. Irregular realizations result in inadequate cash flow and all consequential problems. The working capital cycle can even grind to a halt.

Factoring ensures smooth cash flow and is beneficial to the clients in the following ways:

1. Clients have a liberal debts purchase limit, which will be periodically revised, depending upon business needs. Formalities with the factor are quite simple.

2. While 'Drawing power' under the prepayment limit is revised regularly based on 'Approved debts', actual drawings can be regulated by the client himself, thus saving on discount charges.

3. With the cash flow factor working better than the existing arrangement, a client can be prompt in settling his creditors, avail of cash discounts and improve profits.

4. Sales ledger of the client is maintained by the factor on his computers, and rendered every month.

5. In full factoring, all that the client has to do is Produce, Sell and Forget.

Chapter-VI

Micro, Small and Medium Business Management

6.1. Introduction

The systems of Indian Micro, Small and Medium Business operations are not fully structured. The organizational setup of Indian small and medium business is based on either formal or semi formal or informal system of management. The management of business activities of the small business never follows all principles of Business management. Because, the main reason is that Indian small entrepreneurs are not having proper management education and they are not ready to use the management principles to analysis and take the decisions by using proper scientific management techniques and approaches. Majority of MSMEs are established in rural and Semi Urban areas. The geographical location, usage of traditional production technology and poor financial position of Small Business Organisations are the main pull down factors to procure the management experts for their offices. But those institutions which are having its offices in urban area and using modern production technology are systemized with optimum managerial background. So the relevant principles of business management to Indian can be discussed in this chapter.

6.2. Meaning and Definition of Business Management

The phrase management is defined by experts in management science in different ways. In general, it is a focused and directed activities concerned with accomplishing objectives with and through the efforts of others. It is intangible in the sense; it is a force which is invisible. Its presence is felt in the form of results such as increased productivity, discipline and enthusiasm of subordinates in an organisation. According to peter Drucker, management is "a multipurpose organ that manages a business and manages managers and manages worker and work. The practice of management has a long period. Management discipline as it exists today, evolved over a period of time, and the subject of management is frequently defined in terms of types of things managers should do.

6.3. Management Process of Small Business

The Based on the above discussed definitions, the major process of management of MSMEs are started from Planning of all activities which needs a proper organisational activities with systematic direction. It also consists of Staff management, Communication and Control system, (Table 6.1)

Table 6.1: Management Process of Small Business

Process	Contents
Planning	Future course of actions for a particular period .It is in either monetary or non-monetary terms.
Organizing	establishment of authority relationship with provision for co-ordination between them, both vertically and horizontally in the enterprise structure
Staffing	Manpower acquisition, Retention and maintenance, Compensation Management, Motivation and Industrial Relations.
Directing	Influencing people to direct their efforts towards the achievement of some particular goal
Communicating	Sending and Receiving of messages both horizontally and vertically
Controlling	Setting up the Standard norms for work &task and Controlling the work and Tasks within the Standard

1. *Planning*

It involves thinking and analysis information, arriving at certain assumptions in connection with is likely to happen in the future and then formulating the activities required achieving desired results or goals or objectives. The Planning is Future course of actions for a particular period. It is in either monetary or non-monetary terms. The Planning process ends with master budgets for a single small business for a particular period and department or operation or product wise budgets of the particular enterprise based on Master budgets.

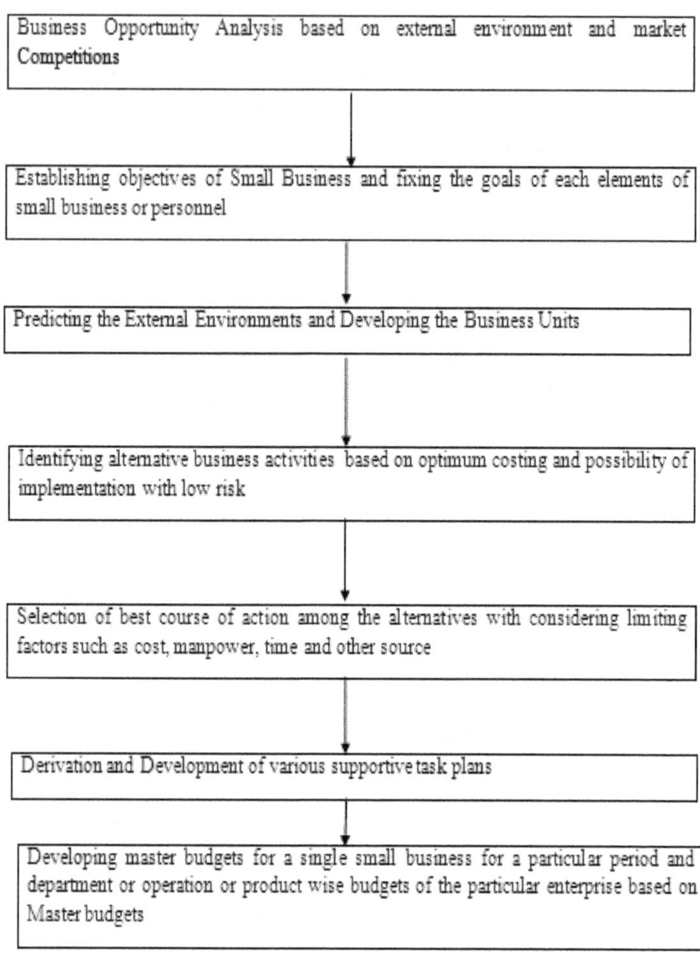

Chart 6.1: Steps in Small Business Planning

2. *Organising*

It involves the establishment of authority relationship with provision for co-ordination between them, both vertically and horizontally in the enterprise structure. According to Halman, Organizing is the process of defining and grouping the activities of the enterprises and establishing the authority relationship among them .In performing the organising function, manager departmentalize and assign activities so that they can be most effectively executed.

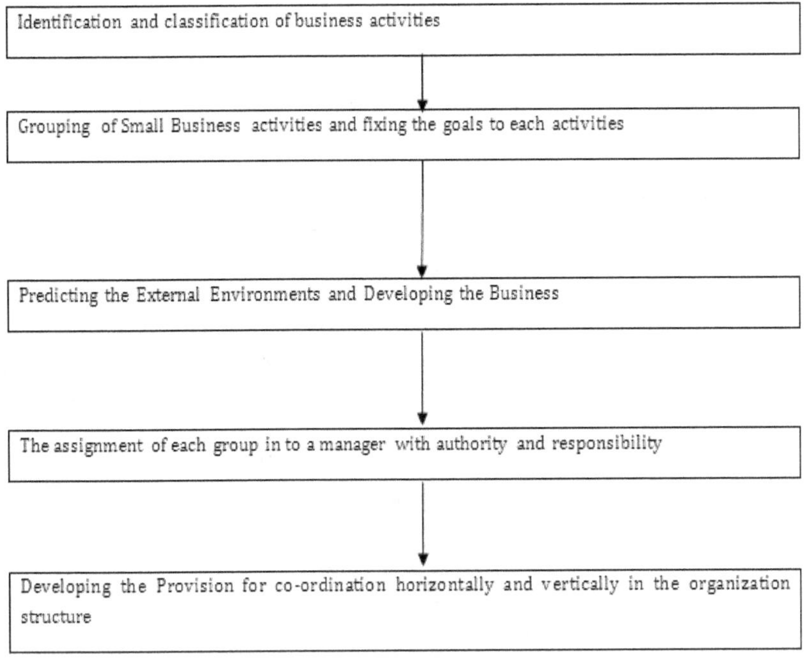

Chart 6.2: Steps in Organising of Small Business

3. *Staffing*

It involves effective recruitment, selection, placement, appraisal and development of people to occupy the roles in the organization structure. It is closely related to organizing that is, to the setting up of intentional structure of roles & positions. It consists of Manpower acquisition, Retention and maintenance, Compensation Management, Motivation of Human resource and Industrial Relations. The scope of staff management in Indian small business organization is very limited one. No one think its staff management as like as multinational companies human resource department. Majority of small business units are functioning without a separate Human resource department with sufficient staff members.(*Ravikkumar.B: 2015,p-1*)

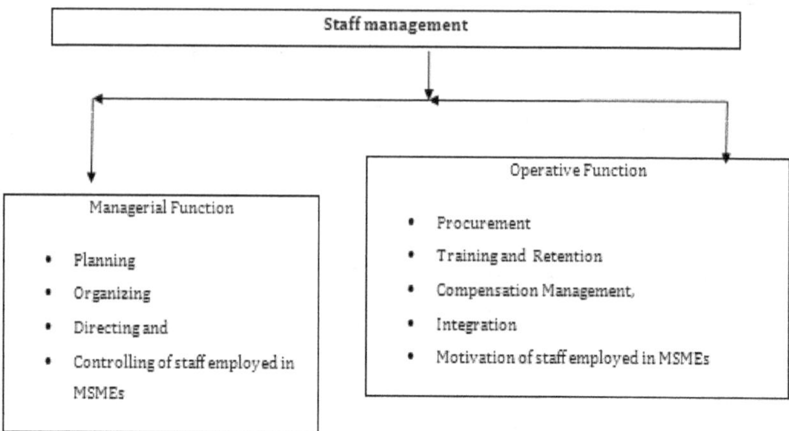

Chart 6.3: Functions of Staff Management

4. *Leading or Directing*

It is concerned with the interpersonal relations of managers and non-managers. Leadership generally is the process of influencing people to direct their efforts towards the achievement of some particular goal.

Table 6.2: Essential Elements of Leadership Qualities of Small Business

leadership Qualities	Relevant Behaviours
Intelligence and Experience	Intelligence and experience are required for keen observation, problem solving, reasoning and decision making for the development of business
Stabled Emotionality	Well adjusted, Small business leaders are free from anger without anti social attitude and free from bias
Socialization skills	Having a better human relation with all segment of peoples
Empathy	Understanding the things and situation from other man's point of view.
Technical and Managerial Skills	Technical knowledge regarding the production and marketing of small business activities and optimum decision making skills
Communication & motivational skills	Sending and Receiving of messages both horizontally and vertically by using both verbal and non verbal communication methods with aiming to motivate the other persons.

Leadership is the ability to persuade others to seek defined objectives enthusiastically the function of planning, organizing, staffing & controlling must be supplemented by people guidance, by good communication and by an ability to lead

5. *Communication*

The managerial functions of planning, organizing & controlling become organized systematically at optimum level only through proper communicative activity. Communication is an interpersonal process of transmitting (Encoding of the messages in communication process) and understanding (Decoding of messages in communication process) through the use of common symbols. It consists of upward (Communication from bottom level to top level), downward (Communication from top level to bottom level, horizontal (Communication between same cadre of peoples) and vertical communication (Communication between different cadre of peoples). The verbal and non verbal methods of the communications are used.

6. *Controlling*

Controlling involves accurate, prompt appraisal of actual operating results, followed immediate prescription and taking of corrective action. These are not 'adopted' but 'adapted' to the particular needs of the firm.

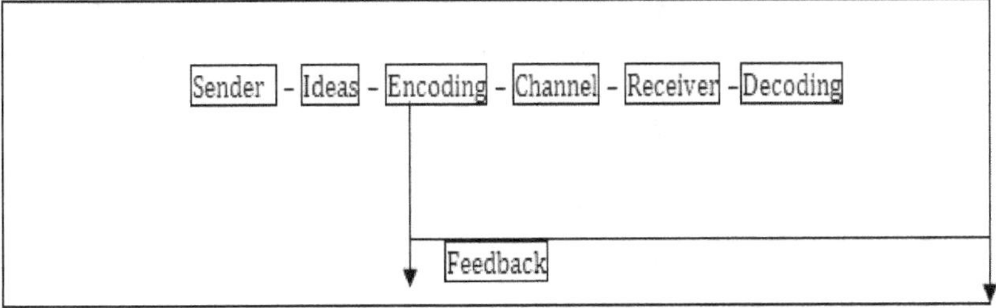

Chart 6 4· Communication Process

6.4.   Functional Area of Micro, Small and Medium Business Management

The major functional areas of management are:

a.   Marketing management.

b.   Financial management.

c.   Staff management.

d.   Production management.

6.4.1. *Marketing Management*

Marketing management is the analysis, planning, implementation, control and coordination of business activities that direct the flow of goods and services from producers to consumers as per the latter's satisfaction and thereby achieves the business objective. Marketing is an orientation, a thinking process, a discipline and an approach to business as well as an organizational function.

1. *Marketing Orientation*

One of the first tasks of an entrepreneur is to make correct decisions regarding the kind of goods or services to be produced which can be sold to the customer.

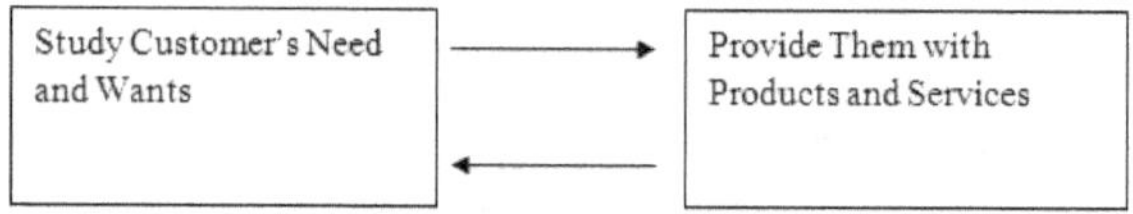

Chart 6.5: Marketing Orientation

Marketing orientation induces thinking about customers and their needs, and assists in creating an appropriate product or service and in selling it. The best way of sensing opportunities for new ideas is to study the benefits that people are buying in a product rather than its physical features.

Why do people go to hill station during summer?

What benefits they are seeking?

- Cool atmosphere
- Relaxation
- Green sight Fun
- Scenery Romance
- Summer festivals.

For instance, in India the desert cooler market grew because many people wanted the cool atmosphere for which desert cooler is much available for longer duration then a visit to a hill station.

Identifying WHY people buy rather then WHAT they buy is essential to successful marketing.

Marketing means that entrepreneurs manufacture what they could sell to the consumer, and not sell what he/she could manufacture.

Marketing orientation' has become increasingly relevant to low technology industries and services such as:

- Wearing Apparel
- Consumer durables
- Transportation
- Grocery
- Health/Beauty aids
- Cosmetic, etc.

Successful marketing depends on the degree to which resources of the enterprise are effectively mobilized to respond to the current and anticipated consumer needs.

2. *Market Assessment*

The market is composed of a wide variety of customers with different backgrounds and spread over wide geographical areas. As the first step, an entrepreneur is required to know the potential of the products or services he wants to offer. It may also be necessary to understand the nature and extent of competition in its marketing and the prevailing trade practices. Such efforts will be helpful in assessing the market. Depending upon several factors like the availability of recourses, the scale of operation, and the impact on profitability, one may decide the customer group, called the market segment, which is of interest to the enterprise.

The market assessment involves three major steps.

A. Analysis of demand;

B. Understanding the competitive situation : and

C. Trade practices

A. *Analysis of Demand*

Demand analysis refers to assessment of the willingness and ability of customers to by product services. Three sources are commonly used to collect information for analysing demand.

i. Primary sources-An enterprise may have household as well as institutional demand for its product. The demand from the household customers is usually met through the dealers and, as such, a rough estimate of the total demands selling the items. Similarly, a number of institutions using the items may be contacted to ascertain the demand. Such personalized contacts with primary sources are possible only when customers are concentrated in a limited area.

ii.   Secondary Sources-In case the potential customers are scattered over a wide area. The published data-regarding population, production, economic condition, living habits, census data and the development plans of the respective state or country are used to estimate the demand.

iii.   Sample survey-When the potential customers are spread over a wide area and are large in number. The information is obtained by sending a questionnaire through mail to a small but representative sample. It may be necessary to consult an expert in drawing the sample and designing the questionnaire.

Elasticity of Demand

Demand at what price? Demand for some products and services is flexible than for others. Demand is said to be **elastic** when a small change in the price affects a large change in the quantum of demand. If a change in price does not substantially change the quantity of demand, the demand is said to be **inelastic**. For a product, the demand for which is highly elastic, a high managerial efficiency is required to maintain price stability.

B.   Understanding the Competitive Situation

Competitive situation demands special attention in the whole exercise in the market assessment. To understand it in respect of a given product/service, an entrepreneur is required to answer questions such as:

- How many enterprises are offering the same or similar goods/services.
- What are their market shares?
- What are the strengths and weaknesses of their products?
- What kind of consumer image does each product enjoy?
- What trade practices the competitors enjoy?
- Who are the major customers of each brand?

The answer to such questions may be useful for understanding the competition. The analysis (SWOT-strengths, weaknesses, opportunities and threats analysis) will tune his marketing efforts to the requirement of the customers and trade by highlighting the areas of opportunities and threat.

C. *Trade Practices*

Trade practices reveal the mode, means and modalities of serving customers with products/services. Due to the spread of customers, or their buying habits or even the nature of the products, it is not feasible for an entrepreneur to reach customer directly. A host of middlemen like distributors, wholesalers, retailers, commission agents, broker, super markets, and export houses are employed to provide various types of services on different terms and condition. A study of the prevailing trade practices in the beginning would enable entrepreneurs prepare a more realistic plan for marketing the product or services.

3. *Market Segmentation*

The market consists of a large number of individuals having different characteristics. They differ in their education employment, income, status, preferences, likes, and dislikes and opinions. Not all of them are potential customers for a product. Through market segmentation, groups of customers are identified sharing some common characteristics and are considered as the target group or segment for the product. There can be many more bases for segmentation such as habit-smoker, non-smoker, etc (Table 6.3)

Table 6.3: Basis of Market Segmentation

S.No	Nature of Segmentation	Basis of Market Segmentation	
1	**Geographical**	Area	Village, Town, State, Country, Hill, Valley, Rural, Urban, etc
2	**Demographic**	Age	Children, Youth, Adult, Old sex-Male, Female
		Income	High, Middle, Low, Below Poverty Line
		Occupation	Executives, Professionals, Farmers
		Education	Primary, Secondary, Graduation ,technical
3	**Psychology**	Attitude	conservative, liberal, radical
		Autonomy	independent/dependent
		Work Orientation-	Hardworking/Soft Working

The identified **segment** must be sufficiently different from the rest to justify calling it a segment. Segmentation is useful and cost effective since it helps selecting appropriate of selling, pricing, packing and promoting the products/service

4. *Marketing Mix*

There are several marketing aspects under the control of the entrepreneur. He can choose the features or attributes of his product, keep its price high or low, advertise it through newspapers or radio, sell it through own salesmen or through retailers, and soon on. In each decision, there are large numbers of possible alternatives. Entrepreneur has to evolve a proper 'mix' of all the decisions areas such as product, price, promotion, and place (popularly called 4 Ps) constitute the 'marketing mix' of accompany. Marketing mix is an essential part of marketing management. It is used as a "tool-kid" for integrating various kinds of marketing decisions to formulate strategy.

Table 6.4: Model Marketing Mix

Target Market segment	Households in high income group, living in urban areas and status conscious
Product	Power inventors incorporating latest imported technology
Price	Optimum Level
Promotion	High, to project a superior quality image of the product. But not high enough to make it out of the reach of those in the lower in the lower bracket of the high income group.
Place (or distribution)	Through sophisticated retailers in selected urban areas

The marketing mix of different companies selling different products is different. A company selling tooth paste will have a different marketing from a company selling industrial tools. These differences are not anomalies. They represent the strategies in the effort to obtain distinctive advantage and competitive edge in the market.

Various elements of marketing mix interact are interdependent. A decision to enhance the product quality will have repercussions on its price: a policy of widening the distribution network will require a corresponding increase in advertising: the introduction of a promotional schemes to win over the competition will require active support from the channel members: and so on.

Moreover if a product is of high quality, it should be through high quality (or reputed) retailers, and advertisements should project and build up the high quality image, thus, a good marketing mix should have logical consistent fit between two or more elements.

5. *Products (Goods and Services)*

Table 6.5: Products Management Process

S.No	Products Management Process	Contents
1	Product Policy	Classification of Products and Services like as Consumer products and industrial products
2	Product mix	The set of all products offered by a firm for sale. It may consist of a single product such as different varieties of soap or more than one product line
3	Packaging	Acquisition of a lot of promotional value for a product
4	Branding	A Word, mark, symbol, or combination thereof used to identify the goods or services.
5	Product service	After Sales Service

It consists of Product policy, product mix, and Packaging, Branding and product services as discussed below

5a. Product Policy

A product is anything that is offered to market for sale at a **price**, it can be physical product like a computer or a service provided by a travel agent.

Types of Products

A. Consumer Products

Goods which are bought by individuals' households without requiring further processing. i.e. soaps, television sets, toys, clothes, and furniture are all consumer products, these consumer goods could be further categorized as:

- Durable goods: which survive many uses and have a relatively long life (e.g. refrigerators, typewriters, fans, etc.)
- Non-durable Goods, which are consumed in one or few uses and last a relatively short period (e.g. soft drinks, soap, cigarettes, etc.)
- Convenience Goods: which are frequently purchased with minimum of efforts in deciding (e.g. newspapers, tooth brushes, etc.)
- Shopping Goods: which have unique features and, therefore, require special purchasing efforts (e.g. sporting equipment, stereo systems, reaching cars, etc.)

Table 6.6: Kinds of Products

S.No	Types of products	Nature of Products and services	Examples
1	**Consumer Products**	Durable goods	Refrigerators, Computers
		Non-durable Goods	Newspapers, Tooth brushes
		Shopping Goods	Sporting equipment, Stereo systems,
2	**Industrial products**	Capital goods	Buildings and Machinery
		Raw material supplies	Inputs like a steel, maize
3	**Services**	Banking	Public sector , private sector banks
		Education	Schools colleges, Universities and specialized institutions
		Hospital	Government and private Hospitals
		Transport	Bus ,train and air ways
		Hotels	Bakery, lodges, Star hotels
		Tourism	Hill areas
		Entertainment	T.V channels, Magazines

B. *Industrial Products*

Industrial products are which are sold to other business firms, either for their own consumption or for producing other goods. They can be further categorized as:

Capital goods, raw material supplies

C. *Services*

There are many services like insurance, transportation, tourism, health care, education, entertainment, repairs etc. As distinct from the normal physical products, one important feature of services is their intangible nature. Some services teaching have very high degree of intangibility while some other like health care have both tangible and intangible components.

5b. Product Mix

Product mix is the set of all products offered by a firm for sale. It may consist of a single product such as different varieties of soap or more than one product line such as varieties of soap or more than one product line such as different varieties of soap and tooth paste. The factors affecting product mix decision are:

- Profits and sales growth potential.
- Stability in sales
- Better customer service
- Utilization of available know-how and other strengths of the company
- Cost reduction
- Better capacity utilization.

5c. Packaging

Packaging over the years, has acquired a lot of promotional value for a product. Many products like cosmetics, playing cards, readymade garments are made attractive to the through fancy and elaborate packaging. Packaging performs several functions including:

a. Production from damage during handling, transportation, storage, etc.

b. Creative a distinctive brand image in the minds of the customers.

c. Providing information about various aspects of the product like weight, name of the manufacture, date of manufacture, contents, etc.

d. Making the product attractive to the customers, Cosmetics filed is an excellent example.

e. Improving the handling, convenience during storage, transport and displaying.

Many new materials and technologies are now available for packaging of different products. While designing the package for a product, a firm should consider the following:

a. The functions which are to be performed through packaging.

b. The practice being followed by the industry.

c. The available of any new materials, technologies or styles.

d. The tastes, preferences, and convenience of the customers; and

e. The costs involved.

5d. Branding

- A brand is word, mark, symbol, or combination thereof used to identify the goods or services.
- A brand name is that part of a brand which can be vocalized (e.g. Gillette, Sony, and citizen).
- A trade mark is that part of a brand which has legal production for exclusive use.

We see that most products that sold today branded. Some of advantages of branding are:

a. It helps in giving a distinctive image to the product.

b. It helps in communicating to the customers some desirable features of the product.

c. It make easy for the customers to order and identify the product.

d. It could help in providing legal protection against imitation.

e. It helps in building a loyal set of customer.

f. It helps in earning goodwill for a company which useful for growth and diversification.

5e.Product Service (After Sales Service)

For many products, there is need for service after they are sold and delivered to the customer. In fact, for products like television sets, computers, and automobiles, the availability of after-sales services is important criteria for deciding the purchase. Companies manufacturing such items spend large amounts of money in making the services available to the customers.

The services include:

a. Installation, maintenance and repairs of the equipment

b. Training of the customers on various aspects of product use: and

c. Provisioning of spare parts.

Provision of goods after-sales service can be used as a strong marketing point in case of many products. It increases the saleability of a product by generating confidence in the minds of the consumers. Moreover, satisfied customers ensure not only repeat purchase but also act as a source of publicity for the firm. Recognizing the importance of after-sales services, many firms emphasise this aspect in their advertising.

6. Pricing

The price of products is the amount of money a consumer must pay to have it, Pricing decisions are extremely important as they greatly influence the profitability of a firm. Moreover, price is perhaps the handiest tool available to a firm to adopt its marketing strategy to changes in demand, costs and competitive situation,

Many factors, both economic and non-economic, influence the pricing decisions.

These are:

- Cost
- Demand
- Competition
- Government regulations
- Behavior of the consumers, and
- The objectives of the enterprise.

Table 6.7: Pricing Methods of MSMEs Goods and Services

S.No	Pricing Methods	Pricing Strategy
1	Cost Plus Pricing	The total cost of the product is fist determined. (Total cost is the sum of variable costs and fixed costs that are attributable to one unit of output). A margin of profit is then added to determine the price
2	Variable price-policy	Policy of charging different prices from different customers depending upon the situation prevailing in the market.
3	Base Price and Discounts	a base price is list price or fixed and varying discounts are offered to different categories of customers
4	Market Rate Method	Price is fixed as the going rate at current market
5	Skimming Strategy	Strategy of setting an extremely high initial price that skims the cream demand. so that investment is recovered in the shortest possible time.
6	Penetration pricing	Strategy of setting an extremely low initial price
7	Odd number pricing	Fixing of price in odd numbers such ,999.99

Some methods and policies which are used individual or collectively in taking pricing decisions regarding pricing are:

A. Cost Plus Pricing

The total cost of the product is fist determined. (Total cost is the sum of variable costs and fixed costs that are attributable to one unit of output). A margin of profit is then added to determine the price.

This method has several advantages:

a. It is easy to operate,
b. The prices can be adjusted according to changes in the costs.
c. The entrepreneurs become cost conscious, and
d. The profitability is known easily.

There are certain disadvantages as well in using this method, since it does not take into account demand aspects, and other external environmental factors.

B. *Variable Price–Policy*

Some entrepreneurs adopt a policy of charging different prices from different customers depending upon the situation prevailing in the market. This policy is usually adopted when the product sold in different market segments. Situation under which the variable price policy is adopted are:

a. Difference in the order size of the customers:
b. Difference in the anticipated business from different customers;
c. Difference in the bargaining power of the customer;
d. Ignorance of the buyers;
e. Difference in the ability to pay.

Under this policy, the minimum price is determined by the total cost of the product. And the maximum price by the customer' ability to pay. Bargaining is normally resorted to finalizing a deal. However, the use of this method may affect the goodwill of the company in the long run.

C. *Base Price and Discounts*

Under the variable policy, the prices are changed according to the particular situation. Under the base price and discount policy, a base price is list price or fixed and varying discounts are offered to different categories of customers. The discounts are offered uniformly to all customers and each one of them can avail these on satisfying the stipulated condition.

The discounts are of several kinds:

a) Trade discount as available to the members of the trade to cover their costs and provide them with a margin as incentive.
b) Quantity discount is available to the bulk purchaser of the product.
c) Cash discount is given to the customers making cash down of immediate payment.
d) Seasonal discount is given to boost the sale of a product during slack season.

D. *Market Rate Method*

If the nature of the product manufactured by affirm is such that is largely indistinguishable from those of the competitors, if it is that found all manufactures are charging more or less the same price for their products, the market rate method of pricing is usually adopted. The price is guide by common in the case of services like courier, tailoring, or car or sector servicing. The advantage of the method, especially for newly established small scale firms, is that they get some immunity from the vagaries of price fluctuation.

E. Skimming Strategy

This is a strategy of setting an extremely high initial price that skims the cream demand so that investment is recovered in the shortest possible time. This strategy is seldom possible except when the product is an innovative one and is accepted to command good reception from the market. It usually requires heavy promotional expenditure. One cannot continue with such a strategy for a long period of time as the competitors would enter the market. The price is permitted to fall as it becomes difficult to maintain abnormally high price in the face of competition.

7. Promotion

Promotion, which is one of the marketing mix, consist of four major components:

a) Advertising.

b) Personal selling.

c) Sales promotion.

d) Publicity.

All these are the tools available to a firm to influence the customers in favour of its product through communication with them.

a) Advertising

Advertising is mass, paid communication under clear sponsorship, the ultimate aim of which is to impact information, develop attitude, and induce action beneficial to the sponsored. The objectives of advertising are to reach a large number of people, and develop a positive disposition of the product or service. The primary goal of advertising is to improve the likelihood of customers buying the advertised product.

Table 6.8: Advertisement Strategies of MSMEs Products

Goal	Functions	Advertisements Media
To improve the likelihood of customers buying the advertised product	To make a announcement of a sales-promotion scheme	Newspapers, Magazines, Trade journals
	To expend the distribution network;	Television, Radio, Cinema (slides of films)
	To counteract the competitors' move	Outdoor-billboards, posters, display, cards (e.g. on buses)
	To build up enthusiasm of the dealers towards the company's products	Yellow pages, Direct mail
	To support the personal selling efforts	Specialty advertising (e.g. Distribution of such items as calendars, shopping bags. Writing pads, etc.)
	To boost the image of the company;	Email and Internet or Telephonic / cell phone advertisement

Besides, it is used to perform certain other functions such as:

- To make a announcement of a sales-promotion scheme.
- To expend the distribution network.
- To counteract the competitors' move.
- To build up enthusiasm of the dealers towards the company's products.
- To support the personal selling efforts; and
- To boost the image of the company.
- Media generally used for advertising are:
  - Newspapers.
  - Magazines.
  - Trade journals.
  - Television.
  - Radio.
  - Cinema (slides of films).
  - Outdoor-billboards, posters, display, cards (e.g. on buses).
  - Yellow pages.
  - Direct mail.
  - Specialty advertising (e.g. Distribution of such items as calendars, shopping bags. Writing pads, etc.).

One or more of these media are selected on the basis of their effectiveness in reaching the advertising message to target customer.

Designing of an Advertisement

While designing an advertisement, what is to be and how it is to be said are of equal importance. The advertisement should be able to persuade the customers to buy a product by conveying to them a persuasive and unique proposition, called 'unique proposition (USP)'. The presentation of the proposition should be such it gives an added force to it.

A check-list for assessing the effectiveness of an advertisement includes:

- Does the advertisement place emphasis on the right things?
- Is the presentation persuasive?
- Is the advertisement interesting to read?
- Is it easy to read?
- Is it able to draw attention?

b) *Personal Selling*

Personal selling is man to man selling and thus, it is a two way communication process between the seller and buyer. Personal selling is used to perform several functions such as:

- Order booking
- Enquiry generation
- Technical assistance to the customers
- Price negotiation
- Collection of payments
- Market information.

Personal selling is extensively used for selling industrial products. In case of consumer products, the role of personal is predominantly to meet the requirements of the trade.

Qualities of Good Sales Man

Salesman in different companies differ widely in terms of their education, skills, and even salaries, some of them are successful and others just perform the duties assigned to them as a routine. Characteristics that distinguish a good salesman from the duties assigned to them as a routine. Characteristics that distinguish a good salesman from the ordinary:

Job Description of Sale Man

1. *Through Knowledge of the Merchandise*

A salesman is supposed to know his subject well. He must be in a position to discuss the advantages, various uses, and special features of the merchandise.

2. *Preparation for Each Visit*

A good salesman plans every visit properly and makes preparations. Previous appointment is helpful in eliciting positive response from the customer. The salesman is ready with all the relevant information and support material that may be required during the meeting.

3. *Understanding of the buyer's Interests*

Selling involves the matching of the interest of the buyer and seller. A good salesman notes and appreciates the viewpoint of the buyer. He anticipates the objections of the customers and provides sound and satisfying answers.

4. *Trustworthiness*

A good salesman generates confidence in the customers through fair dealing, helpful attitude and honouring his commitments. He does not make false claims or give false assurances. Developing trustworthiness takes time but the benefits are lasting.

c) *Sales Promotion*

Advertising provides the customers with a reason to buy a product; whereas sales promotion provides an incentive. There are a large number of sales promotion tools or methods. These may be directed towards the consumers or the consumers or the members of the trade.

Table 6.9: Sales Promotion Activities

S.No	Sales promotion activities	Contents
1	Price offs	Offers a discount in price for a special period.
2	Samples	Distribution of free or subsidized samples
3	Premiums	Offer of an article (e.g. a spoon or a cake of a soap) as an incentive to buy the product.
4	Quantity offs	Offering more quantity of a product at no extra cost.
5	Contests	The consumers are invited to participate in contest or campaigns and are given prizes.
6	Buying allowances	Special discount offered to the trade for a specific period
7	Display Goods	Special display items like racks, banners etc. distributed free to the dealers
8	Advertising Allowances	A part of the expenditure incurred by dealers on advertising is reimbursed
9	Dealer Sales Contests	The dealers are invited to participate in sales contests and win prizes

8. *Place (Channels of Distribution)*

When a manufacturer produces something, it has to be moved nearer to the place of consumption. Consumers may be scattered in large areas and, therefore, a firm usually has to take the help of middlemen to reach them. Basically there are two alternatives available to a firm to reach its consumers:

1.   Direct Selling.
2.   Indirect channel.

Table 6.10: Channels of Distribution of MSMES

S.No	Channels of Distribution	Sequences of Channels members
1	Direct Selling	1. Manufacturer-consumer 2. Manufacturer –Government (Government direct purchase)
2	Indirect channel	1. Manufacturer →Retailer → Consumer 2. Manufacturer → Wholesaler → Retailer→ Consumer

The channels which are used by various firms to reach the ultimate consumers are called Marketing Channels. The various intermediate member of the marketing channel, like wholesalers and retailers are called intermediaries.

Wholesalers are those intermediaries who buy good from the producers and sell them to the retailers or other bulk customers.

Retailer is those intermediaries who sell primarily to the ultimate consumers. They usually sell in lots, and deal in a large variety of products.

A firm should consider the following important aspects while selecting the alternative channels.

a. Nature of the product;

b. Level of its operation;

c. Buying habits of the consumers;

d. The industry practice

e. Dispersion of the consumers.

For the example if the firm making high value capital goods which are sold to institutional customer located in a small geographical area, it can possibly employ direct selling method which has no intermediary.

6.5. Financial Management

The financial management of the MSMEs is a part of management decision making regarding the raise of funds from various sources of funds such as equity capital, Preference share and loan & debentures and utilization of this fund at optimum level through proper accounting and preparation of statement of accounts and also keeping systematic practice of cost and management accounts. Finally, it deals with disbursement of net earnings to the various sources of funds. In this connection, All MSMEs should keep its accounts in proper forms and prepare the statement of accounts and analysis its financial results in proper ways to know its current viability of financial position.

Basic Accounting Mechanics (Book Keeping)

Whenever business transaction takes place, it has to be recorded in a systematic manner. There are three basic accounts books such as Nominal accounts, Real accounts and Personal accounts under double entry system .The journals in which the transactions are recorded. These are the cash book for recording cash transaction; the sales day book (for recording credit sales transaction), and the purchase book (for recording credit purchase transaction), the residual transaction can be recorded in the proper journal. At present Tally soft ware in computer is used to keep the accounts.

6.5.1. Statement of Accounts

Two statements of account are often used describe the performance of an enterprise .i.e.

1. The Balance sheet shows what a firm owns and what it owes at a particular date in terms of assets and liabilities respectively.
2. The Operating statement which is also referred to as profit and loss account. It indicates the performance such as income, cost of sales, gross profit, expense, tax and net profit during a period of time, s These statements are also viewed as legal requirements.

The Balance Sheet

A balance sheet is a statement of a firms owns, and what at a particular date. Things that are owned by a company are called assets, and various sums of money, that it owes, are called its liabilities. Assets include land, building, machinery, stocks of finished goods, raw materials, etc, and anything else that it owns. To acquire these assets, the firm must obtain money various sources like banks or other financial institutions and investors (or shareholders). It may also own money to its suppliers and other individuals. These are liabilities. The total assets always equal the total liabilities. (Table 6.11)

Table 6.11: Model Balance Sheet of MSMEs ltd

Liabilities		Assets	
Current liabilities	Rs.	**Current Assets**	Rs.
Bank over draft	10,000	Cash in bank	2,000
Accounts payable	25,000	Cash in hand	1,000
Interest payable	5,000	Accounts received	12,000
Provision for taxation	3,000,	Securities and deposits	10,000
	43,000	Finished products	
		Work in progress	
		(Semi finished progress)	
Long term liabilities		Raw materials	15,000
Term loan (secured for		Other supplies	25,000
fixed assets) at 12% p.a.	100,000		5,000,
Unsecured loan from	50,000,		78,000
development bank at 15%	150,000		
p.a.			
Shareholders' funds		**Fixed assets**	
Capital		Land	
Earned Surplus		Building	30,000
		Plant & Machinery	45,000
	50,000	Vehicles	80,000
	20,000,	Furniture, etc	25,000
	70,000		5,000
Total	263000	**Total**	263000

6.5.2. *Operating Statements*

One important information for every owner is to know whether a business has earned a profit or during a particular period i.e. the profitability of a business during the period (often one year). The operating statement is also known as profit and loss account. Depending on weather there is a surplus or deficit, the business is said to have earned a profit or incurred a loss during the specific period. (Table 6.12)

Income: The profit and loss account starts with total of all the year the revenues or income earned during the period. For a manufacturing unit, the income is predominantly from the sale of goods.

Profit and loss Account for the year ending --------

Income		
Sales		
Other income		
Cost of sales		
(+)stock January 1,1994		
(+)Purchases		
(-)Stock December.31,1994		
Total cost of goods sold		
Gross Profit		
Operating and Selling Expenses		
Salaries and Wages		
Rent		
Advertising		
Interest paid		
Maintenance & repair		
Total Operating & Selling expenditure		
Profit before tax		
Tax		
Net profit		
Dividends		
Retaining earning or Earned Surplus		

Cost of Goods Sold

The cost of goods sold is computed the price of balanced stock from the total cost of old stock and new purchase during the period. The cost of raw material used during the period is obtained from the records and stock statements. Similarly, the changes in the work in progress and finished goods inventories not shown in the simple profit and loss account given above) must also be taken into account.

Gross Profit

The gross profit or gross margin indicates the profit earned through the manufacturing operation and is derived by deducting the total cost goods sold from the income.

Operation and selling expenses: These are the general administrative, selling and financial expenses, not strictly related to the manufacturing process during the period.

Profit before Tax

By deducting the operating expenses from the gross profit, we arrive at the profit before tax.

Net Profit

When we deduct the tax from the profit before tax, we get the figure of net profit. This is distribution as divided end to the share holders or owners. Usually a portion of the net profit is distributed as dividends and balance is retained in the business as retained earnings.

6.5.3. Cost, Revenue, and Break-Even Point

In many manufacturing establishment, it is essential to identify various cost involved primarily for the purpose of planning and control. For example, the information on the cost of manufacturing a product is highly relevant for pricing decisions. The relationship between the cost and the revenue determines the profitability of a unit.

One way of classifying the cost in a manufacturing organisation is by identifying the direct manufacturing costs and the indirect manufacturing costs. **Direct costs** are those which could be directly identified with the manufactured product. Thus the raw materials consumed in the manufacturing process are part of direct costs. The salaries, and wages and other compensation paid to the workers involved in the manufacturing process are also part of direct costs. **Indirect costs**, on the other hand, are those costs which are incurred for carrying out the manufacturing operations but are not directly identifiable with the end product. Wages paid the supervisory staff, support services and supplies, factory rent, repairs and maintenance expenses, depreciation insurance, tools used and water and electricity for the establishment are all examples of indirect manufacturing overheads. Note that the labour costs may have both direct labour and indirect labour components.

For many kinds of managerial decision, it may be necessary to know the cost associated with a unit of output. In other words, the total cost that is incurred in manufacturing one unit of the product. For this the costs are classified as.

Variable cost which vary in direct or approximately direct proportion. To the Number of units produced (e.g. direct material cost and direct labour cost). Variable costs are determined in terms of per unit of output .

Fixed costs are relatively free of the level of production. Examples of fixed costs are interest charges, administrative salaries, factors overheads, and insurance. Fixed costs are period costs. i.e. they pertain to a period of time rather than to the number of units produced.

Total cost is the sum total variable costs and the fixed costs per unit of output. Suppose the fixed costs, per month of a firm are Rs.5,000 and it makes 500 units or product during this period. The fixed costs per unit of output will be Rs.10. thus the total cost indicates the cost a firm incurs in the manufacture of a unit of output at its particular level of operation.

Incremental cost is the additional variable cost associated with producing one additional unit of the item.

Marginal cost is the additional variable cost associated with producing one additional unit of the item.

Concept of Break-even point: A business incurs costs in anticipation of earning revenue. Revenue is the money it gets in exchange for the products and services its sells. If the revenue in a particular period is more than the costs incurred. We say that the business is said to have made a loss.

The Break–even point is the volume of production at which a firm neither makes a profit nor a loss. In other words, at the break-even point, the revenue equals the total cost the formula for computing breakeven point is simple:

Total revenue (R) = price (P) x number of units sold Q

Total cost C   = fixed cost (F) + Q X variable costs per unit (V)

By definition, at break – even point. R = C

Thus, break-even sales volume =fixed cost/contribution per unit

In the above computation, total revenue and total cost are taken for a particular period. Thus, if the fixed cost is taken for a month, the break-even Sales volume will also pertain to one month's period.

Form the formula for the break-even point; it is clear that a firms break-even point can be lowered by:

- reducing the fixed cost
- increasing the price of the product , and
- reducing the variable costs

From the control point of view, it may be easy to charge a higher price for the product due to the competitive environment in the market. It may be extremely difficult to the alter the variable costs due to the demand supply position. Fixed costs are comparatively more amenable to control and such as area which require prudent planning.

6.5.4. *Working Capital Management*

In addition to the investment in fixed assets, a firm must carry additional cash, inventories, and amount receivables. Once the fixed assets are acquired raw material have to be purchased, process into finished goods, delivered to the customers, and then the payment received as per the terms of sale. This process of consumption and generation of funds takes a definite time and a business has to provide for the funds takes a definite time and a business has to provide for the funds required during this period. This requirement of funds for running the operation of a unit is called its working capital requirement.

The cycle of operation is a continuous one, and as such, a business has to provide for the funds for this cycle perennially. A firm manufacturing one hundred fans per day will require more funds than a firm manufacturing fifty fans per day. The amount of working capital required will also depend upon the length of the cycle of operation: longer the cycle greater are the requirements of funds. For example, if the period of collection of payment increases from one month to two month the firm shall require working capital for additional one month of account receivable.

Under normal circumstances, it is expected that the cash generation (Output) will be more than the cash consumption (input), so that the business is able to meet its obligations regarding interest on loan, dividends, growth. Etc. due to the dynamic nature of business operations, it is extremely difficult to make a precise assessment of its working capital requirements. The requirements changes from time to time.

For the sack of simplicity it may be assumed that all the funds that are consumed during the cycle are required at the beginning of the cycle are required at beginning of the cycle itself. Usually, the requirement of funds for the period of cycle (say, three months) is taken in respect of the following items:

a. Raw materials
b. Consumed like water and electricity
c. Staff and labour
d. Other miscellaneous expenses

It should be understood that the needs pertaining to the working capital are dictated not only by the characteristics of the manufacturing process but also by the characteristics of the market. In many industries, a liberal credit term has to be offered to the customers as a norm: it has ceased to be regarded as a special favour. For example, large institutional customers have their own compulsions and policies to buy their requirements from the suppliers who are able to offer long credits periods. Any assessments for the working capital needs will be more realistic if it is based on such market characteristics.

While assessing the working capital are needs, one must also cater for the marketing expenses. One must learn to treat **Working capital as dependent on the production as well as the marketing activities of an enterprise.** In the case of several consumer products: the funds required for marketing activities may be quite substantial, even more then the production requirements. There are many cases where the entrepreneurs started their operation in small, half-build sheds, spent considerable amount on marketing, and achieved exemplary success. Thus, a realistic assessment of the budgetary needs for marketing helps in arriving at a pragmatic figure for the working capital requirements of an enterprise.

6.5.5. *Time Value of Money of Money*

For investment purpose, a turn of Rs.100 today is more value than a return of Rs.100 after five years. Consequently, the timing of return is extremely important in financial decision making. Let us acquaint ourselves with certain formulae which are based on the **time value of money.**

Compound Interest

The formula for computing the terminal value (A) of an amount (P) invested at an interest rate r per annum at the end of n years is:

$$A = P (1+r)^n$$

Example: if we invest a sum of Rs.1000 at an interest rate of Rs10 compounded annually, its terminal at the end of three years shall be:

$$A = 1000 (1 + .1)^3$$

$$=1000 \times 1.331$$

$$= Rs.1331$$

And the year end of **20 years, 6727.4**

Present Value

Present value implies the value at the present time of an amount of money realized sometime in the future.

This can be found from the same formula which is used for compound interest.

Since,

$$A = P (1 + r)^n$$

$$P = \frac{A}{1+r1} = A (1 + r)_n$$

In this case, P will be the present value of the amount A which we are going to realize after a period of n years at r interest rate.

Example: What is the present value of **Rs. 10000**, to be received after 5 years if the interested rate is **12%** per annum?

Putting values in the formula, we get,

$$P = 10000 (1 + .12)^{-5}$$

$$= 10000 \times .56742$$

$$= Rs. 5674.2$$

Standard Annuity Formula

A serious of even cash flows is called an annuity. The standard annuity problem can be defined as: suppose a man periodically deposits a certain amount of money R with a bank at an interest rate of r per period. How much will be in his account after n such payments?

The standard annuity formula is: $S(n) = F (1 + r)^n - 1/.r$

Where. S(n) is the amount after n payments.

Example 1: if a man deposits Rs.**1000** per annum for **10** years under a recurring deposit scheme carrying an interest rate of **14%** per annum, how much will be get on maturity?

$$S(n) = 1000 (1 + .14)^{10-1}/.14$$

$$= 1,000 (3.7072)^{-1} / .14$$

$$= Rs. 19337$$

(Present value tables are available for computation)

Example 2: how much should a man deposit annually to accumulate Rs.**20,000** in **15** years if interest rate is **12%** compounded annually?

Here we have to find R, THUS

$$20,000 = R (1 + .12)^{15-1} /,12$$

$$= R \times 37.279$$

$$or = Rs.536.49$$

Present value of an annuity

The present value PV of an annuity given by the formula:

$$PV = R(1 - (1 + r)^{-n}/r$$

Where

R= the payment made each period

r= interest rate per period

n=number of periods

Example: what amount should be invested now to receive income of Rs.**5000** at the end of each year for **10** if the interest rate is **12%**

$$PV = 500(1 - (1 + .12)^{-10}/.12$$

$$= 500 (1 - .32197)/.12$$

$$= Rs.28251$$

6.5.6. *Financial Statement Analysis*

Financial statement analysis (or financial analysis) is the process of reviewing and analyzing a company's financial statements to make better economic decisions. These statements include the income statement, balance sheet, statement of cash flows, and a statement of retained earnings. The process involving specific techniques for evaluating risks, performance, financial health, and future prospects of an organization.

Financial statements provide small business owners with the basic tools for determining how well their operations perform at all times. Many entrepreneurs do not realize that financial statements have a value that goes beyond their use as supporting documents to loan applications and tax returns.

These statements are concise reports designed to summarize financial activities for specific periods. Owners and managers can use financial statement analysis to evaluate the past and current financial condition of their business, diagnose any existing financial problems, and forecast future trends in the firm's financial position. Evaluation pinpoints, in financial terms, where the firm has been and where it is today. Diagnosis determines the causes of the financial problems that statement analysis uncovers and suggests solutions for them. Regular preparation and analysis of financial statement information helps business managers and owners detect the problems that experts continue to see as the chief causes of small business failure such as high, operating expenses, sluggish sales, poor cash management, excessive fixed assets, and inventory mismanagement.

By comparing statements from different periods, one cans more easily spot trends and make necessary management decisions and budget revisions before small problems become large ones.

1. *Importance of Financial Statements*

1. Virtually all suppliers of capital, such as banks, finance companies, and venture capitalists, require these reports with each loan request, regardless of previous successful loan history.
2. Information from financial statements is necessary to prepare federal and state income tax returns. Statements themselves need not be filed.
3. Prospective buyers of a business will ask to inspect financial statements and the financial/operational trends they reveal before they will negotiate a sale price and commit to the purchase.
4. In the event that claims for losses are submitted to insurance companies, accounting records (particularly the Balance Sheet) are necessary to substantiate the original value of fixed assets.
5. If business disputes develop, financial statements may be valuable to prove the nature and extent of any loss. Should litigation occur, lack of such statements may hamper preparation of the case.
6. Whenever an audit is required--for example by owners or creditors-four statements must be prepared: a Balance Sheet (or Statement of Financial Position), Reconcilement of Equity (or Statement of Stockholder's Equity for corporations), Income Statement (or Statement of Earnings), and Statement of Cash Flows.

7. A number of states require corporations to furnish shareholders with annual statements. Certain corporations, whose stock is closely held, that is, owned by a small number of shareholders, are exempt.

8. In instances where the sale of stock or other securities must be approved by a state corporation or securities agency, the agency usually requires financial statements.

9. The Securities and Exchange Commission (SEC) requires most publicly held corporations (such as those whose stock is traded on public exchanges) to file annual and interim quarterly financial reports.

2. Financial Statement Analysis Participant Instruments

A. The Income and Expenditures Statement

Business revenue, expenses, and the resulting profit or loss over a given period of time are detailed in the Income Statement. It is also called the Statement of Income and Expense, Statement of Earnings, or the Profit and Loss Statement. This report reflects the company's chosen fiscal year.

B. The Balance Sheet

A Balance Sheet records the total assets, liabilities, and equity of a business as of a specific day. This statement is divided to provide two views of the same business: what resources the business owns, and the creditor and owner investments that supplied these resources. These divisions are generally set up in the two-column account form, with assets on the left, liabilities and equity on the right. An alternative is the one column statement form or report form. It lists assets on top, liabilities and equity below.

C. Reconciliation of Equity

This statement reconciles the equity shown on the current Balance Sheet. For corporations this statement is referred to as the Statement of Retained Earnings or Statement of Shareholder Equity. For limited liability companies it is referred to as the Statement of Members Equity and for Proprietorships as the Statement of Owner's Equity. It records equity at the beginning of the accounting period and details additions to, or subtractions from, this amount made during the period. Additions and subtractions typically are net income or loss and owner contributions and/or deductions. Figures used to compile this statement are derived from previous and current Balance Sheets and from the current Income Statement.

D. *Statement of Cash Flows*

The fourth main document of financial reporting is the Statement of Cash Flows. Cash is the life blood of a small business-if the business runs out of cash chances are good that the business is out of business. This is because most small businesses do not have the ability to borrow money as easily as larger business can.

E. *Financial Ratios*

Financial ratios are a valuable and easy way to interpret the numbers found in statements. Ratio analysis provides the ability to understand the relationship between figures on spreadsheets. It can help you to answer critical questions such as whether the business is carrying excess debt or inventory, whether customers are paying according to terms, and whether the operating expenses are too high. When computing financial relationships, a good indication of the company's financial strengths and weaknesses becomes clear.

6.6.   Staff Management of MSMEs

All factors of production, namely, men, machine, and money are important for the successful running of an enterprise. Managing personal involves assessment of manpower requirement: organising their recruitment and selection: and devising their compensation package and sustaining the motivation.

Table 6.12: Staff Management Process of MSMEs

Process	Contents
Manpower Planning	Numbers of workers needed to a business unit.
Recruitment and selection	Selection of right person to right job
Compensating and motivating employees	Payment of financial and non financial reward for the work contribution of the employees
Industrial Relations	Keeping good relations with management and worker in order to ensure the industrial peace

6.6.1. *Manpower Planning*

To assess the manpower requirement, a number of questions have to be answered:

a.   What kinds of manpower needed?

b.   How many of what kind?

c.   What should be their background, education and experience?

d.   What will be their compensation package and career opening?

Answer to these questions will vary depending upon several things like the **size** of the enterprise, the **nature** of the product, and the **demand** and **supply** position with respect to manpower, the **lotion** of the enterprise, and the **government rules** and **regulations.** A small entrepreneur's business is very simple: because of this, he is commonly referred to as the owner–manager. His manpower planning starts from the requirements at his factory or workshop. Depending upon the process and level of manufacture, he may employ some skilled. Semi–skilled and unskilled workers. If required, he employs a supervisor to look after the various operations at the unit. Work study helps in deciding such members.

6.6.2. *Recruitment and Selection*

Once the manpower needs are identified, the positions are filled through the process of recruitment and selection. The recruitment process requires that the job specification in respect of each of position must be clearly defined.

This information is conveyed to the prospective candidates through

- Word of mouth,
- Employment agencies,
- Vocational institutions, or
- Advertisements.

The small units, especially if it is new, may also convey information about its own activities, objectives growth plans, and any other points of strength to put itself in an attractive situation. Such information should be based on factual data and a realistic assessment so as to avoid raising unfounded expectations in the applicant. If persons possessing the required skills are expected to be available locally or in the vicinity, referrals from the existing employees can be good source of recruiting people.

Selection involves choosing the most suitable person for employment among candidates. The relevant information about the candidates is obtained through:

- Application forms which are designed to elicit the desired information.
- Written tests and exercises,
- Personal interviews, and
- Practical assessment.

The choice of the method (s) of selection depends upon the education qualification of the candidates, and the nature of the job, For example, a skilled worker can be best evaluated through practical assessment in a worker situation rather than through written test or interviews.

Candidates also have their expectations regarding these. They may wish to seek additional information on certain aspects relating to the job such as work content, responsibilities, working conditions, promotion opportunities for long term growth, and degree of job security. The selection process facilities exchange of information between the employer and the employee. The candidates who fulfil the requirements of the job and whose expectations the company is able to meet are selected.

6.6.3. *Compensating and Motivating Employees*

The employees have to be compensated for what they do for an organisation. Besides the salary and perquisites, there are many other things which help in retaining them in the company and sustain their motivation.

a. *Direct Compensation*

Employees expect fair wages commensurate with their skills, experience and job content. Wages should be ascertained on the base of cost of living in the particular locality. These should be revised periodically to account for inflation so that the real wages do not go down over the time. Wages must have a system of yearly increments which should be flexible enough to reward good performance.

b. *Fringe Benefits*

The fringe benefits or indirect compensation that an organisation provides to its employees include insurance against accidents, leave, travel concessions, medical facilities, subsidized meals, uniforms, housing etc.

c. *Promotion*

Employees expect to improve their position in the hierarchy over the time. This improvement in the position is termed as promotion. Promotion helps an employee to feel important and useful to the firm. It enhances his status within outside the organisation. Through promotion, he looks to accomplishing more challenging tasks, including participation in the decision making process.

d. Job Security

One reason why many people are reluctant to join small enterprise even at higher salaries are their apprehension benefits sustainably in the long run.

e. Working Conditions

One primary cause of dissatisfaction of workers is 'the quality of their working life' which includes

- Reasonable hours of work
- A work place
- Rest period
- Tea breaks
- Provisions of a room for recreation, lunch, etc.
- Availability of safety equipment and first aid facilities, and
- Water cooler, lavatory, etc.

These things may not improve productivity, but will help in preventing in preventing job dissatisfaction among workers. The management must also ensure that cordiality and friendliness is maintained between the workers. An environment should be created in which the superiors and senior employees and workers develop mutual respect for each other.

f. Selfless Management

An employer who is alert to the problems of his employees can create a happy and motivated work force. A small firm has an advantage that the employer can be close to the employees and any complaint and irritants is more or less instantaneous. Timely praise for good performance evaluation is more motivating the employees. The attitude of the management should be fair and positive in evaluating performance.

In most countries, there are government rules and regulations which govern the employee-employer relations, these may to 'minimum wages' ' leave salary', 'holidays', 'medical benefits', 'bonus',' maternity leave', 'workers', right to form a union' and so on. The policies with respect to the workers must be formulated within the frame work imposed by such rules and regulations.

6.6.4. *Industrial Relations*

The term industrial Relations denote the collective relationship between management and employees in an industrial organisation. Individual relationship of workers with their management is thus excluded from the scope of industrial relations and from part of personal management. Good industrial relations mean absence of disputes between them. Good industrial relations are necessary for the following reasons:

1) To help in the economic progress in the country.
2) To help in establishing and maintaining true industry democracy this is a prerequisite for the establishment of socialist society.
3) To help management both in the formulation of informed labour relations policies and in their translation into action.
4) To encourage collective bargaining as a means of self- regulation.
5) To help government in making laws forbidding unfair practices of unions and employers.
6) To boost the discipline and morale of workers.

6.7.   Production Management

Effective management of internal operations are being recognized as crucial to the growth of organisation. The additional capital requirement   is the thrust area for the introduction of new technologies and creating additional production capacities in several key sectors of economy. The need for optimum utilization of the resources becomes extremely important. Nowadays, the focus is also shifting from looking at the operation of a company and their efficient management to be broader objective of quality and customer service and of making tangible contribution to economic growth.

Production and operation management concerns itself with the conversion of inputs into output, using physical resources, so as to provide the desired utility/utilities of form, place possession etc. to the customer while meeting the other organizational objectives of effectiveness, efficiency and adaptability.

Operation management or systems is managing productive resources/systems in efficient manner. It takes into account the principle of managing the productive systems and contains an element of planning and controlling. Re-engineering is a recent term for operation management.

The production and operations management function can be classified into the following four areas:

a. Technology selection and management
b. Capacity management
c. Scheduling/Timing /allocation and
d. Systems management

6.7.1. *Production Planning and Scheduling*

Any operation, whether it is in a manufacturing or a service enterprise, requires detailed planning about supplies, work and maintenance. Based on market assessment and segmentation, a sales forecast products for the ensuing year may be prepared. Accordingly, the requirements of man hours, capacity utilization of machines and inputs needed for manufacturing products are offering services are estimated. The supply of inputs, raw materials, tools and spares are planned indicating the source, Period and mode of procurement. The plan of supplies should have flexible to suit the changing customers' requirement.

The production work need to be planned considering the type of line flow where the production goes in sequence changing the all the items until the final product emerges. Batch production, where components are produced in batches by resting them. Job production is one where the product is manufactured as per customers' specification.

The work should be planned to use maximum capacity of machines and provide work for each workman so that he does not have to wait for any job. Similarly, there should be sufficient workers to cover all machines and functions (simultaneously or in sequence).

Maintenance is planned best by drawing a preventive maintenance schedule where the machines will be stopped in a staggered and pre-planned manner. The important aspect of planning is that work should not stop when needed.

Production planning and control is the means by which a production planning is determined. Information issued for its execution and data collected to plan control at all stages.

The successful production control is attained through four steps:

1) Plan the rout based on the standard capacity of each machine, decide how must load put on each (85% capacity utilization is considered good)

2) Scheduling and instruction procedure to ensure that all concerned know what needs to be done and by what time.

3) Availability of material required and supplies as per the schedule : and

4) Monitoring i.e. to compare the plan with actual events, outputs and stocks. Careful analysis will show that some work can be brought back on schedule by making a few changes by using the spare capacity of these machines that are ahead of schedule.

6.7.2. *Inventory Control*

A business unit requires to keep inventories of raw materials, goods in progress (semi-finished goods), and finished goods, both in stock and in transit. It has many advantages:

1) Materials are readily available when required for production/use.

2) Quantity discounts result in large orders.

3) The finished goods inventory allows a firm to meet the requirements of the customers promptly.

4) The demand may fluctuate over time and finished goods inventory helps in reducing the impact of such fluctuations on the process of production.

However, "holding the inventory" has certain costs; a balance has to be reached. To decide to order an inventory, one has to decide;

a) Order lead time: Average time that elapses between placing an order and receiving the goods;

b) Usage rate: the level placing an order and receiving the goods;

c) Usage rate: the level at which a new order must be placed so that the inventory is replenished before the stock reached zero level (stock out).

Recorder Point

A re-order point is estimated by using the formula

Recorder point = Usage rate X Lead time.

Suppose a company uses **10** units of an item per day (usage rate), and the order lead time is **15** days, a new order must be placed when the inventories level reaches **150** units (recorder point **150** = usage rate **10 x** lead time **15**) so that the inventory is replenished before a stock out occurs.

The Inventory Techniques

a. Economic Order Quantity

To determine how much to order, a concept called the Economic Order Quantity (EOQ) is used. Though maintaining large inventories involves carrying costs, the placing of an order also involves order, processing costs consisting of the cost of materials (stationary, stamps etc.) and purchase establishment expenses. If the ordered quantity is large, an order has to be placed less often. The total order-processing costs increase when the size of the individual order is reduced and carrying costs increase when order is quantities increased. The EOQ is a point in which all the cost are at optimum level.

$$EOQ = \frac{\sqrt{2AB}}{CS}$$

A = Annual requirement

B= cost per units

C= Ordering cost

S = Carrying cost

The inventory

b. ABC Analysis

To know which items constitute the bulk of the value of total inventory a technique commonly known as the ABC analysis is used.

It has been observed that out of a long list of inventory, a relative small percentage, approximately **20 %** lock up a major **share (70-80%)** of capital. Whereas relatively small cost (say **5%** of capital) is used to buy the bulk of the items in the inventory. These items, which occupy small volume (**20%** and account for the major capital **(70-80%)** are termed 'A' category items.

Another **20%** of the items may account for the **10-15%** of the total value and are termed 'B' category items.

The remaining **60%** of the items which account for only about the total value are termed 'C' category items.

Steps Involved in ABC Analysis

1) For each item calculated the cost (number of pieces)
2) Arrange these items in progressively decreasing order
3) Calculated and write the cumulative total cost in their column
4) Then compute the % of cumulative total to
   a) Total cumulative and
   b) Total number of items and record **a+b** in column **4 & 5** respectively.

Each item under category A is crucial to an organisation in terms of inventory control, purchase efficiency, and working capital management.

6.7.3. Purchasing of Raw Materials

It is estimated that, on the average, a manufacturing company spends about half of its sales income on the purchase of materials and components. It is said that "a dollar saved is a dollar earned". A company which fails to see the value of a "dollar saved may soon be out of business

Purchasing function is performed by buying materials of the right quality, in the right quantity, at the right time, at the right price, and from the right source.

This is done by:

a) Pursuing : open document policy:
b) Maintaining proper inventory records regarding stock at hand, detailed specifications, sources of supply, re-order quantity, purchase price, usage rate etc. in case there are large number of purchase items, then ABC analysis may be required.
c) Developing good vender relationships to ensure emergency supply , scope to modify an order, readiness to bear with delayed payments arising out of financial exigencies and finally to be sure about the quality of supply,
d) Creating alternate sources of supply to minimize the chances of stocks outs, dependency on single supplier who may start directing and avail benefit of cost reduction as per prevailing market price.

6.7.4. *Quality Control*

Quality refers to the intended use and the price of a product. A technically excellent product may be prohibitively costly, and there is no point in making a product that the customers cannot afford to buy. Quality, thus, is a relative term and must be viewed as such.

When a company decides to manufacture goods of a particular quality level, it must ensure that this level of quality is maintained consistently. In technical terms, the variations in the quality of products must be kept within the specified tolerance limits.

- Prevention of the occurrence of a fault.
- Detection of as soon as it occurs, and
- Rectifying it at the earliest.

For attaining quality standards there, must be clearly stated standard with reference to raw materials, components, workmanship, packaging performance and all other benefits that customer expecting from the goods and services. Quality testing and measuring equipment of the required specification should be considered as essential components of the unit. Various methods like 100% inspection, spot checking, and inspecting as per a sample plan are used for quality testing. Under sampling plan, only a portion of the incoming material is inspected. The number of items to be inspected or the size of the sample is determined statistically.

If the finished product is a high value item, 100% inspection is usually carried out so that no substandard product reaches the customers. A stamp of quality approval is affixed on each item. In some cases even destructive tests like impact testing, and test for resistance to fire also carried out on a small fraction of the items. This should be considered as investment rather than wastage. While the benefits, both tangible and intangible, of quality control are many, there are also costs involved in the process. As the quality control is made rigorous, the costs tend to increase. One has to strike a balance between the costs and benefits arising out of quality control needs of a particular organisation.

ISO 9000 Series Standards

The international Organisation for Standardisation (ISO) is the specialized international agency for standardisation, at present comprising the national standards bodies of 91 countries including India. ISO is made up of approximately 180 technical Committees. Each Technical Committee is responsible for one of the many areas of specialisation. The object of ISO is to promote the development of standardisation and relate world activities with a view to facilitating international exchange of goods and services and to develop cooperation in the sphere of intellectual, scientific, technological and economic activity.

The result of ISO technical work is published as international standards.

With increased focus on quality issues worldwide, various standard developing organisations prepared standards and guidelines in the quality field. Although there were similarities among the many standards, the quality picture became quite cloudy. Terms such as quality Management, Quality Control, Quality System, Quality assurance, and quality Policy, had acquired different, and sometimes conflicting meaning from country to country, within a country, and even within a industry. Standardisation was needed at the international level. Work was initiated within the international organisation for standardisation (ISO) and in 1987 six standard where issued: one on standard terminology, and five standards   (known as the ISO 9000 series) which clarify the relation between different quality concepts and present three models for quality assurance systems.

ISO 9000 standard series tells suppliers and manufactures what is required of a quality oriented system. It does not set out extra special requirements which only a very few firms can or need comply with, but it is a practical standard for quality systems which can be used by all Indian organisations.

ISO 9000'is an opportunity and a challenge to developing nations. They can now know with a good degree of certainly the level of quality that purchasers expect. They also can learn the prerequisites and characteristics of good quality assurance and quality management. The challenge to a developing nation is to motivate processors and manufactures to adopt and implement these standards, and to establish a credible national quality registration scheme which will be recognized by trading partners.

In an increasing number of markets and industries, third-party quality assessment and registration is becoming a pre-requisite for doing business. ISO **9000** registration is considered the minimum acceptable level for a supplier, and those who cannot demonstrate the minimum level may not only have difficult in selling in certain markets; they may be barred from those markets. A supplier without ISO **9000** registration can face higher insurance rates, or be denied insurance in some markets.

In addition ISO **9000** series standards also:

- Motivates exporters
- Sets a base line
- Establishes reasonable standards for Government procurement
- Focuses training and professional development
- Sets general market procedure for regulating health and safety

- Reduce time–Consuming audits by customers and regulators
- Improve their quality image
- Gives marketing advantage and EC92 positioning
- Raise levels of motivation, cooperation, workmanship, and quality awareness
- Improve efficiency; reduces scrap and rework.

While the ISO **9000** quality standard were written to be used in voluntary or two–party contractual situations, they are fast becoming pre-requisites for doing business in Europe and other regions. ISO 9000 conformance is becoming pre-requisites' for market entry, product certification, and laboratory accreditation. ISO **9000** is being incorporated into buyer/seller agreements, ISO **9000** quality management standards will have considerable impact in markets through the world.

ISO **9000** series standards are available with Bureau of Indian standards and the standards are known as IS **14000** to IS **14004 (BIS)**. They are available from their headquarters in Delhi and branch offices all over India. Entrepreneurs can address their enquiries to:

Director-Sales,

Bureau of Indian Standards,

Manak Bhavan,

9, Bahadur shah Zafer Marg,

New Delhi – 110 002.

Registration of ISO Standards

ISO **9000** registration means the certification of company quality systems by third party through their mechanism of registration. European customers expect Indian companies to have their quality systems registered to ISO **9001**, **9002** and **9003**. This is generally done by having an accredited independent third party on–side audit of your company's operations against the requirements of the appropriate standard. Upon successful completion of this audit, your company will receive a registration certificate that identifies your quality systems as being in compliance with ISO **9001**, **9002** and **9003**. Your company will also be listed in a register maintained by the accredited third party registration organisation. You may publicise your registration and use the third-party register's certification mark on your advertising, letterheads, and other publicity materials

Chapter-VII

Preparation of MSMEs' Project Report

7.1. Introduction

A project is the integration of various resources of 4 Ms (men, money, material & machine) to achieve an objective. A project report is a synchronization and synthesis of relevant data in respect of a project which serves as a guide to management and record merits and demerits in allocating resources to productizing on of specific goods or services. It is prepared for analysing the form of opportunities in the contemplated project.

A project report gives a complete analysis of the inputs and outputs of the project. It enables the entrepreneur to understand, at the initial stage, whether the project is sound on technical, commercial, financial and economic parameters.

7.2. Significance and Scope

A project report spells out how production should be organized to yield maximum results. It is also referred to as pre-investment feasibility study' or a 'Business plan' that describe in detail what business one want to be in, and, how the business will achieve the stated goals, and, when would that happen. It is an operating document.

A project report highlights the practicability of project in terms of different factors like economy, finance, technology and social desirability. It is needed by entrepreneur for carrying out expansion or starting a new production line and for getting loans from financial corporations, banks and other financial institutions.

An important aspect of the project report lies in determining the profitability of the project and minimum risks in the execution of the project.

While preparing and presenting a project report the following major aspects need to be addressed.

1. *Economic Aspects*

The project report should be able to present economic justification & market analysis for investment. It should present analysis of the market for the product to be manufactured.

Market analysis is basically an exercise in answering three questions viz.

a) How big is the present market?

b) How much is it likely to grow, if at all?

c) How much of the future market the contemplated project can capture after allowing a margin for future entrants?

It provides an analysis of the economies of production.

2. *Technical Aspects*

The project report should give details about the technology needed, equipments and machinery required and the sources of availability of plant and machinery.

3. *Financial Aspects*

The report should indicate the total investment required. It should also highlight the sources of finance and the entrepreneur's contribution. It should present a comparison of cost of capital with the return on capital.

4. *Production Aspects*

It should contain description of the product selected for manufacture and the reasons for such selection. The report should also bring out the fact whether the product is export worthy. It should also give details of the design of the product.

5. *Managerial Aspects*

The report should contain qualifications and experience of the persons to be put on the management job. If the entrepreneur will look after management, the report must emphasise as to how he is qualified to manage the venture.

A project report analyses product characteristics, demand outlook, competition, distribution channels and practices, the financial implications and requirements of personnel.

Agencies for Preparation of MSMEs Project Report:

1. Small Industries Service Institute (SISI)
2. The Micro, Small and Medium Enterprises–Development Organization (MSME-DO) [earlier known as SIDO]

An entrepreneur can himself prepare the report, or, it can be prepared by a consultant. There are several organizations which help the entrepreneurs in the task of preparation of reports.

7.3. Contents of a Project Report

The following are the contents of project report.

1. Objective and Scope of the report.
2. Product characteristics (specifications, product uses and application, standards and quality).
3. Market position and trends (installed capacity, production and anticipated demand, export prospects and information on import and export, price structures and trends).
4. Raw materials (requirements of raw materials, prices, sources and properties of raw materials).
5. Manufacture (processes of manufacture, selection of process, production schedule and production technique).
6. Plant and machinery (equipment and machinery, instruments, laboratory equipments, electric load and water supply arrangements, sources and availability of plant and machinery).
7. Land and building (requirement of land area, building, construction schedule).
8. Financial implications (fixed and working capital investment, project cost and profitability).
9. Marketing channels (trading practices and marketing strategy)
10. Personnel (requirements of staff, labour and expense on wage payment).

7.4.   Project Report Format

1. *Summary*

   1.1 What is being proposed?

   - Product/service
   - Location
   - Ownership
   - Project cost

   1.2 What is wanted?

   - Funding pattern including term loan and capital loan requirement
   - Assistance regarding technical collaboration

2. *Introduction*

   2.1. Description of product

   2.2. Details of applications of the product

   2.3. Latest trends of product.

   2.4. Rationale for project selection

   2.5. Product idea

3. *Background of the Promoters*

   3.1. Educational qualifications of the promoters

   3.2. Experience and background

   3.3. Project related experience

   3.4. Investment potential

   3.5. Suitability for manufacturing the products

   3.6. Similar information about any other key persons associated in promoting the project.

   3.7. If the state is one of the promoters, and if the project has international ramification with respect to marketing, technology etc., the information regarding similar projects promoted by the state is to be provided.

4. *Status Report*

4.1. No. of existing units

4.2. Performance of existing units in general

4.3. Installed Capacity and capacity utilization of the units

4.4. Current status of the industry in the country

4.5. Current status of the industry in the international scene (if the proposed project is to operate at international level in terms of marketing.

4.6. A write up on what will distinguish the proposed project from others already operating in the market place.

5. *Market Survey*

5.1. Market potential analysis

- Major end uses of the product
- Available substitutes in the market
- Major buyers
- Purchase decision influence
- Major attributes of similar products if available in the market
- Competitors status at the regional / national / International level (if the project is expected to market the product in the international market)
- Strengths and weaknesses of competitors
- Strengths of the proposed project
- Trade practices adopted by the competitors
- Trade channels adopted by the competitors.

5.2. Proposed approach towards marketing

- Are to be covered–regional, national, international.
- Distribution channels to be adopted.
- Trade Practice.
- Strategy for entering the market and promoting sales.

5.3. Import (from other cities/towns)

5.4. Product mix and new varieties

5.5. Demand analysis and scope for new units

6. *Technical feasibility*

6.1. Manufacturing process

6.2. Process flow chart

6.3. Details of technology

- Indigenous of imported
- Arrangements for technical know-how.
- Availability of alternative Technologies.
- Evaluation of these technology alternatives.
- Possibilities of change in the technology in the course of time and methods proposed to adopt such changes.
- Various process parameters.

6.4. Production programme

- Time required to make one unit of the product
- Input–output ratio
- Any National or International standards set for the product quality

6.5. Selection of plant and equipment (Annexure-1)

- Capacity of plant and machinery.
- Equipment balancing.
- Suppliers.
- Cost.
- Various alternatives available.
- Criteria for choosing the proposed equipments amongst several alternatives.

6.6. Raw material specification & requirement (Annexure-2)

- List of raw materials needed.
- Quantity needed.
- Quality specifications.
- Sources of procurement.
- Cost o raw materials.
- Any tie-up arrangement for procurement.
- Availability of alternative raw materials.

6.7. End product Standards

6.8. Quality control to be used

6.9. Inventory control

7. *Raw Material Requirement*

Capacity Utilization

I st Year   :

II nd Year   :

III rd Year   :

8. *Location of the Unit*

8.1. Exact location of the project

8.2. Various alternatives available which have been examined

8.3. Criteria for selecting the location

8.4. Location advantages like raw material availability, markers, financial benefits and incentives provided by the government, availability of skilled labour, availability of power etc.

9. *Infrastructure Requirement*

9.1. Land, total area requirement and its cost

9.2. Building, total built up area required and its cost, layout

9.3. Power requirements in terms of KW

9.4. Requirement of water, fuel, effluent disposal etc.

10. *Manpower Requirement*

10.1. Requirement of skilled, semi-skilled personnel

10.2. Requirement of technical and non-technical personnel

10.3. Requirement of administrative/managerial staff and marketing personnel

10.4. Position regarding availability of manpower and standard rates of wages, salaries and other benefits to be provided.

10.5. Any scheme for training skilled manpower, if they are not readily available.

11. *Cost of Project and Means of Finance*

11.1 Cost of fixed assets:

- Land
- Building
- Plant & machinery (including electrification installation)
- Furniture/fixtures etc.

11.2. Working Capital Requirement and Margin Money: (Annexure-3)

- W.C. requirement calculated for first 3 years on proposed capacity utilization
- Prices of various raw materials taken on what basis
- Accounts receivable calculated on what credit period and stock of raw materials for how many days.
- What percentage available from bank, own equity, subsidy etc.

11.3. Preliminary and Preoperative Expenses.

12. *Financial Viability of the Project*

12.1 Profitability analysis (Annexure–5)

- Profitability has been calculated on what capacity utilization and no. of shifts in operation for first 3 years.
- Reasons for taking low capacity utilization
- Prices for various raw materials, trade, discount and adv. Expenses etc.
- Interest on long term loan and short term loan. (Annexure–4)
- Depreciation at what rate on Plant & Machinery and Building. (Annexure-6)

12.2. Break-even analysis (Annexure–7)

12.3. Analysis of cash-cum-funds flow statements (Annexure–8)

13. *Government Approvals*

Necessary government approvals are to be obtained. Clearances from government and other regulatory agencies for setting up of the project–what are they and what is the status with regard to obtaining such clearances?

14. *Key Elements for the Success of the Industry*

Annexure 1

List of Machines & Equipments

S.No	Name & specification of machine	No.	Cost per machine	Total

Electrification, transportation & C.S.T. etc.

Annexure 2

Sources of Raw material, Plant & Equipment

Annexure 3

Working Capital & Requirement

S.No.	Items	No. of days	Years of production		
			I	II	III
1.	R.M. Stock				
2.	Work-in-progress				
3.	Finished goods stock				
4.	Accounts receivable				
5.	Working expense (Power + fuel + water + wages + Salaries + admn. Expenses) ___________				
6.	Total W.C.				
7.	Credit available against raw material				
8.	Net working capital requirement				
9.	Short term borrowings from bank @ - %				
10.	Margin by the entrepreneur				

Interest Cost Calculation

Year of production	A	B	C	D	E	F
I Year						
II Year						
III Year						

A: Long term loan outstanding

B: Repayment till date

C: Interest on long term loan @ - %

D: Short term borrowing from bank

E: Interest on bank borrowing @ - %

F = C + E

Annexure 5

1. Profitability Analysis

(Fig. in 000)

Particulars	I Year	II Year	III Year
Annual saleable production			

a) Manufacturing Cost

1. Raw Material
2. Utilities
3. Wages & Salaries
4. Repairs & Maintenance
5. Stores & spares
6. Packing
7. Others

b) Overhead Expenses

8. Rent and Taxes
9. Insurance
10. Selling Expenses:

    (total trade discount on sales)
11. Admn. Expenses

12. Depreciation

13. Interest

14. Total Cost of Goods Sold (a+b)

15. Income from Sales and Waste

16. Profit Before Tax (14-13)

17. Investment Allowance @-% on P & M

18. Taxes

19. Net Profit

---

2. *Financial Ratios*

i. *Debt Equity Ratio*

Debt equity ratio denotes the level of term loan raised per particular amount of equity.

Formula:

$$\text{Total cost or project} = \text{Term loan} + \text{equity} + \text{subsidy}$$

$$\text{Debt Equity Ratio} = \frac{\text{Total Debt}}{\text{Total Equity}}$$

Generally, Debt Equity Ratio should be 2:1 or 3:1

It should not be more than 3:1

ii. *Net Profit Ratio*

It is also known as margin or net income percentage which indicates rate of net profit earned on sales. Formula for calculating Net profit Ratio is as follows:

$$\frac{\text{Net Operating profit}}{\text{Sales}} \times 100$$

iii. *Return on Investment*

This is most important ratio which indicates efficiency of capital employed and its profitability. The quantum of profit has a great relationship with the investment made in the business and this is shown in terms of percentage of profit on the total investment. Formula for calculating Return on Investment is as follows:

$$\frac{\text{Net profit}}{\text{Total Capital}} \times 100$$

High return on investment shows that the investment is very profitable.

iv.   Debt Service Coverage Ratio

It ensures that the internal funds generated would be able to service the equity (i.e. interest to be paid on term loan)

Formula:

$$\frac{\text{profit After Tax} = \text{Depreciation} + \text{Interest (excluding on WC)}}{\text{Interest} = \text{Loan Instalments}}$$

Annexure 6

Depreciation Calculation

On straight line method

S.No.	Name of the assets	I Year	II Year	III Year
1.	Land			
2.	Building @ - %			
3.	Plant & Equipment @ - %			
4.	Dies/Tools			
5.	Furniture/Fixtures			
Total				

Annexure 7

Break–Even Analysis

Break-even point is the level of production to which the total revenue matches the total cost of production i.e. no profit no loss

$$\text{Formula: BE=}\frac{\text{Total Fixed Cost}}{\text{Contribution}}$$

Contribution = Total sales – Variable Cost

Fixed Cost

In does not vary with increase or decrease in production costs like :

- Rent, salaries of executives & office workers
- Insurance
- Certain taxes and depreciation

Variable Cost

It would vary with increase of decrease in production costs like

- Direct raw material
- Direct labour
- Power
- Commission to sales man
- Travel expense

Annexure 8

Cash-cum Funds Flow Statement

Pre-production	l Year	ll Year	lll Year

A) Sources of Funds

1. Profit before taxes with interest
2. Capital or owner's equity
3. Long term loan from financial institution
4. Deposits
5. Depreciation
6. Working capital borrowings from banks
7. Subsidy

B) Uses of Funds

8. Preliminary & pre operative expenses
9. Increase in capital assets
10. Increase in current assets
11. Interest
12. Repayment of long term loan
13. Withdrawals
14. Taxation provision

C) Opening Cash balance

D) Surplus balance (A-B)

7.5. Product Selection

The first step in a feasibility study and project planning is the proper selection and demarcation of the field in which, one seeks to work. The selection of product is to be done after need analysis which must take into account the following factors:

- Who will be the consumers, and, to what categories they belong?
- What will be the dimension of the total market and also of each segment?
- What is the present state of competition in the market?
- The trends in the economic conditions of people, and , the recently introduced changes in government regulations, which are likely to influence the use of the product.

There often exist recommendatory or statutory standards which a product should fulfill (In India, Indian standards Institute lays down such standards. These are popularly known as ISI standards, which are available product wise.)

It is useful to state, right in the beginning, the production capacity one proposes to install. A back-of-the-mind awareness of such proposed capacity will give an idea of, how in-depth a market study is needed. For assessing plant and machinery, and other physical facilities, and late, for financial viability calculations, installed capacity is the most important parameter.

7.6. Location Criteria

The choice of location to establish a project has to take into accounts primarily, the following factors:

i.   Price of land

ii.   Investment subsidy and tax-concessions offered to entrepreneurs by the government for setting up small scale units in specified areas.

iii. Availability of physical and commercial facilities to run an enterprise.

One has to consider a gamut of points while deciding upon a location. The choice of choosing a site–the specific piece of land is also a task, as sometimes, the location-selection and site-selection are so-intertwined that one may drop a location for want of a good site.

Once the location/site is identified, it is useful to evaluate it, in terms of the following checklist to ensure that a major error is not made by the entrepreneur.

The Checklist given has the following six dimensions:

1. The basic considerations (status of development of the town and its location with reference to enterprise needs)

2. Physical Infrastructure Position (Power, Water, etc.)

3. Commercial Infrastructure Position (Telecommunication, banking etc.)

4. Social Infrastructure Position (Housing, Health etc.)

5. Financial Incentives position (Income-tax concession, Investment Subsidy, etc.)

6. Specific considerations with reference to the Site selected (Land Price, Contours etc.)

The entrepreneurs need to put down their findings against each point in the checklist before passing the final comment on any location.

The checklist is as follows.

7.6.1. *Checklist for Location and Site Selection*

Basic Considerations: Dimension I

1. Location (City/Town/village)

2. Population

3. Nearest large city (name and Distance)

4. Connections to major cities (Rail, Road, Air-distance, Connection, Frequency)

5. Climate (minimum/maximum temperature, humidity, etc.)

6. Distance from important geographical markets

7. Distance from major raw material sources and significance (or lack of it) of enterprise proximity to such sources.

8. Distance and connection to relevant ports (in case of export/import oriented enterprises)

9. Manpower : availability of required skills and prevailing wage rates

10. Overall industrial relations (strike/lockout/dispute in the area)

11. Law and order position in the area

12. Level of industrial development in the area.

13. Composition of industrial development in terms of types of industry and size/health of existing enterprises.

14. Proposed enterprise and government preference for type of industries at proposed location.

15. Whether ready built-up factory shed is available at the location and whether its size conforms to the need.

Physical Infrastructure Position: Dimension II

1. Land : Availability and Price
2. Existence of an organized industrial estate.
3. Water-Supply: Source (river, canal, tube well), distance, quality (pH, Hardness), rate, common storage facility, operating authority (Public Works Department, industrial estate authorities, corporation, municipality).
4. Power Supply: Nearest substation, feeder type (industrial/rural).
5. Effluent-Treatment and Disposal (if relevant); Disposal point (land, sea, river), arrangement for treatment (individual, common), drainage arrangement for conveying the effluent (open, underground) treatment and conveyance charge.
6. Approach road/internal roads
7. Street lighting
8. Responsibility for maintaining roads, drainage and street lighting.
9. Annual maintenance charges.

Commercial Infrastructure Position: Dimension III

1. Telecommunication (availability of new telephone connections, manual or automatic exchange, STD facility, Telex facility, etc.)
2. Postal and telegram facility
3. Banking facility
4. Transport-operative facility
5. Weighbridge
6. Typing/Photocopying
7. Courier
8. Warehousing
9. Nearest offices of law-enforcing agencies (excise, sales tax, labour laws, factor, inspection, pollution control etc.).
10. Nearest Offices of Industry–assisting agencies (State Finance Corporation, Industrial Estate Corporation, Raw material/Marketing Corporation, District Industries Centre which sanctions and disburses financial incentives).
11. Building/Electrical/Fabrication facility.
12. Building material, spare parts etc.
13. Motor-rewinding, painting, gas-supply and such other industrial services.

14. Technical educational facility (Industrial Training Institute, Polytechnics, etc.)

15. Professional resources position (management/industrial consultants, financial/legal advisers, management/productivity associations).

Social Infrastructure Position: Dimension IV

1. **Housing:** Availability, Quality, price (ownership and rent), Public Housing (Actual and Planned housing by State Housing Board, Infrastructure Corporation or such other agencies).

2. **Education:** Primary, secondary and university education facility (quality, number of seats, ease of admission, medium of instruction).

3. **Health:** Hospitals and Dispensaries.

4. **Recreational Facility:** library, parks etc.

5. **Hotel Accommodation**

6. **Service Organizations:** Rotary club, Lions club etc.

Financial Incentive Position: Dimension V

1. Investment subsidy (from the Govt.)

2. Income-tax concession.

3. Sales tax exemption/interest-free sales-tax loan.

4. Promoter contribution (margin) and interest-rate policy followed by Financial institutions.

5. Electricity-duty exemption, local-tax exemption and such other incentives.

Site-specific Consideration: Dimension VI

1. Whether the proposed site is a part of an organized industrial

2. Direction of town-growth with reference to the site.

3. Non-agricultural status of the site.

4. Site-contours (leveled, hilly, pits, ravines, brick-kilns)

5. Site-shape (regular/irregular)

6. Immediate proximity of railway line, National highway, state highway.

7. Overhead telephones or power lines or underground water/drainage/ age line passing through the site.

8. Access to National/State highway or other roads direction in relation to the site.

9. Wind direction in relation to the site.

10. Soil-type.

7.7. Plant & Machinery (Identification & Considerations)

The complete ranges of machines and equipments required to carry out manufacturing auxiliary operations have to be identified by the entrepreneur and, the capacity and technical features of individual machines have to be specified. Before drawing up a list of machinery, it is essential to arrive at 'make or buy' decisions and also what to make and what to buy decisions.

Purchase of old machinery must satisfy the required conditions and it is advisable to check the policy of term-loan organization before deciding to acquire second-hand machinery.

The sources of plant and machinery are given by those who provide technical know-how. However, there are directories of machinery manufactures brought out by term-loan organizations, industry associations and research organisations which can be utilized.

The machinery supplier can be selected on the basis of supplier-to-supplier comparison which normally rests on the following considerations:

- Technical features of equipment offered by individual suppliers
- Reliability of equipment offered by individual suppliers
- Price of equipment offered by individual suppliers
- Delivery period stipulated by individual suppliers and their respective reputation in terms of delivery schedule fulfillment
- Nature of warranties or performance guarantees offered by individual suppliers
- Scope of after sale service, terms and conditions of such service and reliability of such service offered by individual suppliers.

7.8. Technical Feasibility and Technological Know-How

The concept of technical feasibility denotes adequacy of the proposed manufacturing process and plant and machinery to produce a given product largely within the frame work of predetermined quality-specifications, raw material and utility-consumption levels and output quantity per 8 hour norms, without long or expensive break-down problems. In order to accomplish technical feasibility, one must make sound technical arrangements. For a small scale unit, the technical arrangements normally are over the following:

- Laying down the manufacturing process.
- Working out the specifications of plant and machinery, identifying possible sources of supply, evaluating offers from various suppliers and formulating a machinery procurement-cum-erection plan.
- Preparing a factory layout plan and assessing built-up area requirement.

- Estimating raw material and utility (power, water, fuel) consumption norms, selecting equipment-systems required to ensure a satisfactory supply of utilities and assessing capital expenditure required to install such equipment/systems.

- Coping with anti-pollution law.

Technical know-how is a fund of knowledge to carry out the above mentioned and related technical tasks. Depending on the technology-content of an enterprise, seeking assistance from a specialized technical consultant may be contemplated, or the technical know-how may be borrowed from abroad (there are instances, rather rate of a small enterprise). This is called foreign technical collaboration. There are legal provisions in force from time to time which specify products for which such collaboration is contemplated, one must check the policy/legal provisions. The provision of technical know-how in case of foreign collaboration normally encompasses supply of equipment, drawings, erection, support, training of Indian manpower by the collaborator etc. In such collaboration agreement, it is important to ensure that all mutual obligations are spelt out comprehensively and carefully.

7.9.   Techno-Commercial Work on Raw Materials

A fair amount of techno-commercial work will have to be done by the entrepreneur on the raw materials aspect which must cover the following:

1. Identification of raw materials required for producing the proposed product.
2. Stating clearly the specifications of all such raw materials.
3. Analyzing raw material loss at each stage of production process.
4. Indentifying all chemicals, stores, consumables and packing material required for producing the proposed product.
5. Working out the consumption norms in respect of raw material, chemicals, stores, consumables and packing material per unit of output.
6. Identification of bought-outs required, the rate at which required per unit of finished output, the price of bought-outs and the names of prospective suppliers.
7. Stating whether (Which) raw materials are available indigenously or imported.
8. In case of imported raw materials, describe the clearances/licences required and thus giving an idea regarding ease of import.
9. Stating names and addresses of major suppliers of raw materials.
10. Ascertaining the (prevailing) price of various raw materials, chemicals, stores, consumables and packing materials.
11. Adding taxes, freight, duties, excise, octopi and such other charges to the price.

12. Ascertaining the credit-period which suppliers normally grant to the buyers.

13. Stating whether there is a price control on raw materials. If so, the details of such control.

14. Commenting on the availability of major raw materials-whether these materials are easily available or are occasionally or continuously in short supply.

15. Stating whether there is a distribution control in respect of raw materials. If so, give details pertaining to registration status, quota allotment expected and so on.

16. Incidence of loss of material in transit or storage, if such incidence is significant.

7.10. Computation of Working Capital

In addition to the investment in fixed assets, a firm must carry additional cash, inventories, and amounts receivable. Once the fixed assets are an acquired, raw materials have to be purchases, processed into finished goods, delivered to the customers and then the payment received as per the terms of sale. These processes of conversion requires the fund. This requirement of funds for running the operations of a unit is called its working capital requirement.

The following check list may be used to compute the working capital in a project report:

1. The expected capacity utilization or output (in physical terms)

2. The quantity of raw material required to produce the above output and the unit price of each raw material.

3. The quantity of raw material which must be carried, given first production target (i.e., carrying level)

4. Ascertaining the value of raw material which the enterprise will keep in stock.

5. Carrying out the same exercise in the case of stores, spares, consumables, packing materials and arriving at the value of these which the enterprise will keep in the stock.

6. Estimating the value of goods in process which the enterprise will carry at any point of time (This depends on the length of manufacturing cycle).

7. Estimating the level of stock of finished goods which the enterprise will generally carry. (This may depend on whether it produces against orders or in anticipation of demand).

8. Segregating total sale as cash only and credit sales. (production cost of sales may be considered here)

9. Determining the amount required to meet a month's wages and salary bills.

10. Determining cost of fuel, light, power and other utilities for a month.

11. Administrative and selling expenses and repairs and maintenance for a month

12. When 4, 5,6,7,8,9,10 and 11 are added, the gross working capital requirement is arrived at. Against all permissible components (except nos. 10 & 11), credit 8 generally granted by banks up to 70% of total requirement, which, however, differ from component to component and project.

7.11. Project Cost Components Analysis

The project cost components are Land & Building, plant & machinery, equipments, other fixed assets like furniture, office equipments etc., preliminary and pre-operative expense, technical know-how fees (including training cost), margin for working capital and contingency and escalation (generally at the rate of 10% of Land & Building, plant and machinery, and other fixed assets).

Preliminary and pre-operative expenses include:

- Cost of feasibility report, consultation fees.
- Project establishment expenses.
- Salary and administrative cost during implementation period.
- Loan application processing fee and mortgage in respect of loan.
- Stamp duty, legal expenses.
- Training cost.
- Interest during implementation period.
- Security deposits for telephone and electrical connections.
- Insurance during implementation period.
- Trial product cost.
- Inauguration expenses etc.

7.12. Cost of Production and Profitability Projection

For estimating cost of production and profitability over a period the following factors are to be considered:

1. Variation in cost of raw materials.
2. Selling price corresponding to variation in the cost of production.
3. Individual and descriptive workout and separate depiction of all cost elements.

Hence, the exercise of preparation of cost of production and profitability statements amounts to compilation of the data already gathered, or processed and presenting the same in a particular format. A suggestive format indicating various elements of cost of production and profitability statement is given below. Depending upon the nature of business, the structure of the format may be modified. *(Table -7.1)*

7.13. Project Implementation

An Entrepreneur has to essentially draw a time-table or an implementation schedule for his/her enterprise. An implementation schedule is an aid to ensure timely implementation of the plan. The task of preparing such a schedule forces one:

i.   To enumerate the various steps which have to be taken prior to commencement of commercial production.

ii. To appreciate the inter-dependence among these steps and hence the chain-effect of delay in carrying one step on overall implementation schedule.

iii. To work out a calendar for bringing in one's own funds for implementation.

Timely implementation is important because, delay in implementation, will cause among other things, a project cost overrun. In order to avoid such adversaries, drawing up a schedule and adhering to it, becomes an important part.

While formulating implementation schedule, entrepreneurs have to bear in mind the following major considerations:

1. He/She will like to carryout tasks involving capital expenditure only after the term-loan is sanctioned.

2. Some tasks are sequential. For example, machinery can be installed only after it is received. Some tasks are not sequential and can be carried out simultaneously e.g. electrification of factory building and recruitment of man power.

Implementation progress entirely is not in his/her hands. An unhelpful official can hold up the term-loan sanction, (e.g. A transport strike may delay delivery of machinery by a few weeks; a loan sanction from a financial institution may take 3 months). Thus, it is important to work out a realistic schedule and to build a sufficient margin of safety. (Table 7.2)

Table 7.1: Cost of Production and Profitability Estimation Format

Operative year	I	II	III	IV	V	VI	VII	VIII
A. Material Costs								
a. Raw material								
b. Components								
c. Consumables								
d. Packaging materials								
B. Utilities								
a. Power								
b. Water								
c. Fuel								
C. Labour and Plant Overheads								
a. Direct wages								
b. Factory supervision salaries								
c. Bonus, provident fund, gratuity								
Total labour cost								
D. Factory overheads								
a. Repairs and maintenance								
b. Rent and taxes								
c. Insurance								
d. Miscellaneous factory expenses								
e. Contingency								
E. Estimate of cost of Manufacture A+B+C+D								
F. Administrative Expenses								
a. Administrative Salaries inclusive of Gratuity, P.F., etc								
b. Remuneration to Directors								
c. Professional fees								
d. Postage, telegrams and telephones								
e. Insurance and taxes on office property								
Total administrative expenses								
G. Selling expenses and Sales promotion								
a. advertising								
b. Packing								
c. Selling commission								
d. Taxes/excise duty								
e. Royalty								
Total cost of selling & Sales Promotion								
H. Total cost of production : =E+F+G								
I. Selling price total sales								
J. Gross profit before interest =(I- H)								
K. Financial Expenses								
a. Int. on L.T. loans								
b. Int. on working capital								
c. Guarantee commission								
Total financial exp.								
L. Depreciation W.D.V.								
M. Operating profit = J - K – L								
N. Other income if any								
O. Preliminary expenses written off								
P. Profit / loss before taxes = M + N – O								
Q. Provision for taxes 20%								
R. Profit after tax								
S. Net cash accruals (L + M + O + P)	I	II	III	IV	V	VI	VII	VIII

Table 7.2: Implementation Schedule

Task Month	0	1	2	3	4	5	6	7	8	9	10
1. Study of business plan											
2. Submission of term-loan Application											
3. Term-loan sanction											
4. Negotiations and Securing possession of land											
5. Building constructions											
6. Tie-up with supply Utilities (power, water etc.)											
7. Placing order for Machinery											
8. Receipt & Installation of Machinery											
9. Recruitment of key Manpower											
10. Trial production											
11. Commencement of Commercial production											

7.14. Factors to be Considered While Formulating A Project Report

1. Financial-performance projection must be based on true premises. Over-optimistic and simplistic assumption with reference to utilization of installed capacity should be avoided. The assumptions should take into account the performance of existing enterprise, market conditions, level of competition and the possible technological changes.

2. Adequate attention must be paid to the computation of installed capacity (i.e., capacity calculation). There are several factors which have to be considered like periodic shutdown, down time, capacity of other equipments etc, which tend to lower the overall installed capacity.

3. Stray opinions and unrealistic conclusions about the market should be avoided. The market study component of project report which entails a less structured probe and contend with less definite variables should note a neglected task. One must ensure that it provides accurate information on demand-supply and the market potential, for the position chosen.

4. Faulty decisions on machinery selection must be avoided. Proper and prompt machinery-suppliers have to be identified and care must also be taken on choosing machines for the production of quality products.

5. The technical feasibility must be ensured. There are products which call for sophisticated technology or, are not amenable to being produced in the small–scale sector. Alternatively, it may not be possible to set up an enterprise with a lined-up complete technology within the stipulated financial resources (i.e., lack of technical feasibility). Any shaky arrangement for technology-oriented products will cause the enterprise fore-doomed to failure.

6. In project-pruning and resource-straining, the safe limits should not be exceeded. An entrepreneur may have a definite amount of money to be invested. There may raise an entrepreneurial tendency to accommodate enterprise-parameters within such limit, even if it is not possible to do so. Hence, he/she may cut down the built-up area or exclude some machinery to keep the project cost down, within his own financial limit. He/she may make the most favourable assumption on means of finance (75% of project cost to come as loan). While some amount of economy or optimism may be in order, this is sometimes carried out to such extreme lengths as to render the enterprise-proposal technically unviable or unrealistic (because important facilities are missing and in terms of proposed financial resource plan). Such idea should not be pursued. The technical viability should not be distorted.

7. The preliminary and pre-operative costs and working capital margin must be considered by the entrepreneurs. The project's cost and own resource requirement (margin) should not be underestimated. There entrepreneur must also bear in mind that, if the working capital margin is large, financial institutions will expect the entrepreneur to raise his/her own contribution to project cost.

8. Errors in location selection must be avoided. Entrepreneur should not be swayed by the offer of financial incentives (Subsidy, income-tax concession etc.), neglecting other criteria for location selection. This sometimes becomes the sole and overriding concern. They must take a comprehensive view in selecting a location.

9. Utmost care must be taken in fixing the selling price of the products manufactured. Selling price estimate must be realistic and it is advisable to follow a conservative approach while estimating selling price.

10. The cash flow during implementation period and the initial years must to be charted out in detail. The financial institutions may expect entrepreneurs to spend from their own resources in the first place, and there are machinery suppliers and others who may expect advance payments. Such payments have to be envisaged under the cash plan in order to avoid a halt in implementation.

Chapter-VIII

Establishing Micro, Small and Medium Scale Enterprises

8.1. Introduction

Every enterprise, be it large or small begins as an opportunity identified, defined and assessed. Before setting up an enterprise, one has to go through the exercise of assessing the market demand of the output, be it a service or a product. The market assessment for small scale enterprise will give an idea of the basic marketing concepts involved and the methods that can be used to assess market potential for the product or service. Sometimes, application of particular technology or the possibility of exploiting vocational advantage itself may present an opportunity for successful entrepreneurial ventures and become the cause for setting up small units.

The choice of appropriate technology and selection of site for the units are important managerial decisions.

8.2. Opportunity Identification

Opportunity identification is one of the major activities in which entrepreneurs engage themselves. The term opportunity also covers a product/service or project and its identification is the base for establishment of a business unit.

In identifying a business opportunity an intending entrepreneur is required to understand the environment in which he would operate. The government policy and the market for a product/service should be the first, to be taken for examination. Environmental scanning and assessing strengths and weaknesses in relation to opportunities (SWOT Analysis) in the market and the competitive threats are the major tools which entrepreneurs use in this activity. These are important tools in identifying an opportunity and are generally employed in the working of a business unit.

Literature on management discipline particularly those areas which deal with business policies, strategy formulation, strategy implementation and corporate planning offer useful insights into managerial processes which are at times close to entrepreneurial pursuits which help in adopting a step-by-step account of how an entrepreneur should undertake opportunity identification activity.

8.2.1. SWOT Analysis

SWOT Analysis is an important tool in the identification of business opportunities. SWOT Analysis runs parallel to the enumeration of why small business units are established and How are they established?.

The factors leading the individual entrepreneurs to set up small business units are various like:

a) His/her love for doing business independently

b) The scope small business provides for taking initiative, organizing activities and a kind of freedom which owner-managed small units alone can offer.

c) Self-employment being an income generation activity, as an alternative to wage employment and

d) The presence of operational flexibility in a small unit. Etc.

In the Indian Small Scale Industry, typical small scale units are setup by entrepreneurs by identifying an opportunity which reveals that:

- Entrepreneurs select products based on their own experience or their partners experience in the line.

- Entrepreneurs select products based on the expansion/diversification plans of their own or any other on-going business known to them.

- Entrepreneurs select products whose imports are banned or controlled by the government. This factor has been found applicable in identification of opportunities in small, medium and large scale industrial units.

- Entrepreneurs select products which show high profitability;

- entrepreneurs select products based on certain specific advantages of those products such as, reservation of product lines for small scale units, certain regions or locations;

- Entrepreneurs select products lines guided mainly by changer in certain aspects of industrial policy-more specially change in control and regulation of prices of raw material or products.

- Entrepreneurs select products lines as a result of reports by government committees on policy. Entrepreneurs' selection of computers or electronic products can be attributed to recent approach of government policy to these products.

From these factors one say that the opportunity–product or service–appears to emerge through an interaction between the immediate or related environment of the entrepreneurs to the somewhat remote or unrelated aspects of environment. An opportunity envelope appears to take place with positive and negative or favourable and unfavourable factors attached to different opportunities. This envelope tells how an opportunity is finally identified by an entrepreneur.

8.2.2. *Opportunity Identification Process*

Entrepreneurs pass through several processes in identifying an opportunity, some leading to enchantment and others to disenchantment. At one stage he/she may like the opportunity, at the other, may turn his/her mind to another. However, there are 2 stages which can be clearly identified. At the first stage, the entrepreneur tries to generate ideas or opportunities and in the second stage he/she identifies the opportunity, In the first stage, most of the entrepreneurs are likely to encounter a situation resembling the "Hen or Egg" controversy. Experienced entrepreneurs make use of their experience, background, Contracts, observations, information obtained from friends, development agencies, government policy, schemes of concessions and incentives to generate ideas to be examined as opportunities. They also employ the method of generating ideas about a few projects in order to decide on the most suitable project.

Once a list of opportunities has been prepared, the next activity is to select the final opportunity or project. This can be described as "zeroing in process". The stages through which the entrepreneurs pass through may be described by expressions such as, "Entrepreneurial scanning for projects", "Entrepreneurial selection matrix", "Entrepreneurial rambling" etc.

8.3. Selecting the Final Project / Opportunity Selection

The final selection of the project should follow the course of action adopted in the previous stages and also the examination in detail of each of the areas such as market, raw materials, total investment–amount and technology of plant and equipment–location and the type of organization i.e. ownership, partnership etc. The inter relationship between each of these areas are also to be fully worked out. This can be almost a continuous "back and forth" process wherein, one will be moving from one area to the other.

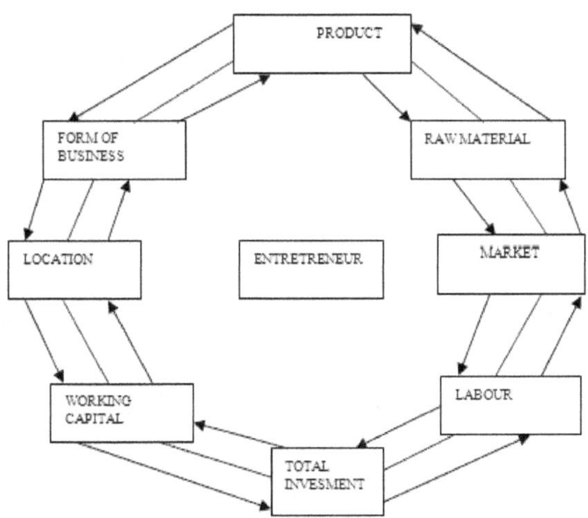

Chart 8.1: Opportunity Identification Process

The most important areas examined in details are:

1. Demand and market
2. Investment
3. Plant and machinery and technology
4. Working Capital
5. Total Investment
6. Raw material availability-indigenous or imported and the price
7. Cost-volume–price relationship and
8. Location of the project.

These areas are closely interrelated and cannot always be examined independently.

Clues on how to Use the Framework

1) As per the financial strength, the entrepreneur may put high, medium or low
2) Competition could be stiff or moderate
3) Could be easily or not easily available
4) Could be favorable or unfavorable
5) Could be again favorable or unfavorable
6) Acceptable – Not acceptable

The overall assessment is thus an outcome of subjective and objective factors relevant to each product/service line. Finally, this step-by-step approach permits the entrepreneur to select his/her opportunity.

8.4. Project Formulation

Project formulation is the process and steps through which an opportunity becomes a project in which the individual is willing to invest his time, money and other resources. In this process the potential opportunity is examined from the point of view of becoming the opportunity and the opportunity must be transformed into a business.

The business opportunity implies a series of activities in which one will decide to invest his/her time, money and organising ability. In other words, it is an opportunity "Worth investing in". An opportunity which is likely to be accepted as final opportunity or project will have the following components:

a) Demand, marketing component

b) Costing and pricing component

c) Financial component in term of term-loan and working capital

d) Location component

e) Merchandise, raw material and process, manufacturing component i.e production component.

8.5. Promotional Policy and Opportunity Identification

The government's industrial policies are promotional programmes help intending entrepreneurs in opportunity identification and setting up of MSMEs units in the following ways.

i) Identification of Opportunities	a) Reservation of products for exclusive manufacture by MSMEs
	b) Government purchase programme for products of MSMEs
	c) Liberal financial assistance for term-loan and working capital
	d) Availability of infra-structure facilities like shed, water, power, roads etc.
ii) Setting up an enterprise	e) Facilities for acquiring machinery on hire-purchase basis, allocation of scarce raw materials etc.
	f) Marketing assistance.

These promotional measures must be added to entrepreneurship and self employment development programmes with different target groups such as unemployed youth, women SC/ST group, rural youth etc. The entrepreneur must identify of his/her own opportunity to set up a small unit on self employment basis. The list of official measures and other programmes of assistance and authorities engaged are discussed in chapter-II.

8.6.   Opportunity Evaluation

In the whole process of opportunity sensing and identification, the promotional policies need to be integrated at every stage along with the analysis of opportunity, strength & weaknesses. An intelligent & experienced entrepreneur would evaluate an opportunity as follows:

1) How large is the gap between demand and supply in the market and what is the nature of competition in the market for the product?

2) Whether the product is covered under any of the promotional policies of the government, so that, either entries into business or competition in the market are facilitated.

3) Whether there is any special product/service specific problem that he/she will face and can avail of any part of promotional policies, to soften the impact of these problems.

Based on all such product-market-policy, policy-market type of analysis, the entrepreneur will finally conclude that the opportunity is **worth-investing-in.**

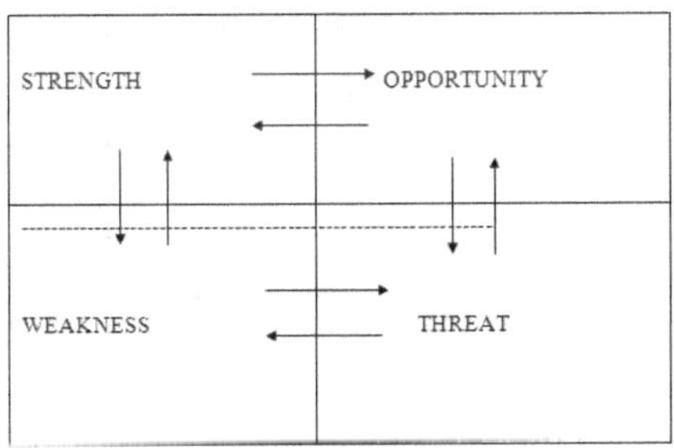

Chart 8.2: SWOT Analyses

The objective and subjective sides of an opportunity are represented by the four rectangles and the dotted lines which enlarge strengths and opportunity can be due to

i.   The policies which help new first generation entrepreneurs and hence add to their strengths

ii.   Reservations of products to be manufactured by SSI's and other policies may enlarge the field of opportunities & counteract that of threats.

8.7.   Market Assessment

8.7.1. *Market Orientation*

Industries whether small or large operate in an environment of controllable and uncontrollable variables. A small enterprise has to interact constantly with the market in which it has to operate and other environmental factors. Its marketing efforts must stay fine tuned to suit the requirements of the market in general and the needs and wants of the customers in particular. In the light of intensified industrial activities, increased competition and customers becoming more discerning, MSMEs' industries have to develop marketing orientation in their outlook, to be successful.

The approach relies first on finding out what the customers want, and then, creating and developing products or services that satisfy their satisfy their wants.

The efforts should be directed to create a product that satisfies the wants of the customers rather than to change their wants to suit the product. The issue is not to produce something, but to produce according to what is wanted by the customers.

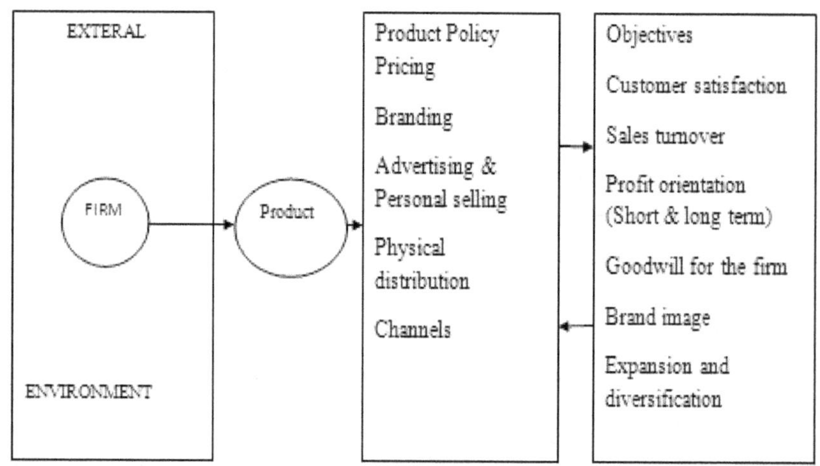

Chart 8.3: Marketing Orientation

8.7.2. Need for Market Assessment

The marketing orientation outlook will force an entrepreneur to seek answers to many questions relating to market segments, marketing inputs, product quality, price structure, technology of manufacture etc., before setting up the venture. This exercise will enable him/her to move ahead with greater degree of confidence and confront the problems that may arise during the later stages, in a professional manner.

Analysis of market demand, the competitive situation and the trade practices are important for a sound market assessment.

The market is composed of a large variety of customers who differ in their likes and dislikes, options, preferences, education, employment, income and status. The location of the customers also differ, some may be located nearer and others in distant places. Depending upon several factors like resource availability, scale of operation and the impact on profitability, scale of operation and the impact on profitability, one has to decide the target segments which are of special interest to the firm. The identification of the customer groups helps in marking an estimate of the market demand for the product chosen.

Once the market demand for the product is estimated, one has to look for the competitive situation prevailing in the market as a firm cannot just pursue its own policies without regard to what the competitors are doing. The nature and extent of competition will put several constraints on the marketing policies of a firm and detailed analysis of the competitive situation will help in pricing and also in identifying the gaps and opportunities that will be available for exploitation.

8.7.3. Market Demand Analysis

A firm is normally concerned with the demand for the product in a particular market or its own area of operation. In that sense, the term market demand for a product can be defined as, 'the total volume that would be brought by a defined customer group in a defined geographical area in a defined time period in a defined marketing environment under a defined marketing programme' (Philip kotler 1988). From the above definition, it is clear that there are eight elements or variables which must be understood by an entrepreneur in order to determine market demand for a product.

They are:

1. Product class or type of product
2. Physical volume of product in terms of units sold, quantity, in monetary terms or both.
3. Market demand of a product that is of interest to the firm which is to be measured for the customer group.
4. The geographical boundaries within which market demand is to be measured must be clear.
5. Demand estimation must be for a specific time period.
6. The external environmental factors which influence market demand.
7. The controllable environmental factors which the firm uses to the demand for their products i.e. marketing programmes or marketing efforts.

8.7.4. *Analysing Competitive Situation*

As the nature of competition may vary from market to market, the entrepreneur needs to analyze the competitive situation with reference to the chosen market segments. Answers to the following questions would help him to assess and understand the competitive situation.

1. How many competitors are there in the marker?
2. What are their market shares?
3. What are the strengths and weaknesses of their products?
4. What is the kind of image competitor's product enjoy from their customers?
5. What trade practices are being adopted by the competitors?
6. Who are the major customers of each competitor's brand?

8.8. Site Selection

In order to minimize total cost of production and distribution of goods, any new organization has to make the major strategic decision on locating its facilities. The selected site must also maximize revenue and provide an opportunity for further growth & expansion In involves a sequence of decisions. The general procedure as proposed by William J. Stevenson consists of the following steps:

1. Determining the criteria for evaluating location alternatives such as revenue increase, Community service etc.
2. Identifying important factors such as market location, Materials availability etc.

3. Developing location alternatives.

   i) Identifying the general region for a location.

   ii) Identifying a small number of community site alternatives.

4. Evaluating the alternatives and selecting the location.

Entrepreneurs face many location problems like location of a manufacturing unit, a warehouse etc., which require the selection of a suitable site. An important assumption made in such a single facility location problem is that revenue, costs and other facility characteristics of the firm do not depend on the location of other facilities for the firm or its competitors. Such a single facility location can be evaluated by qualitative factor rating method and location break-even-analysis

8.8.1. *Qualitative Factor Rating*

The procedure for qualitative factor rating consists of the following steps.

1) Identification and enlisting relevant factors.
2) Allotting a weight to each factor to indicate its relative importance (weights may total 1.00) among the factors considered for decision making.
3) Establishing a common numerical preference rating scale (0-100 points) to all the factors.
4) Scoring each potential location based on comparison with other potential locations.
5) Multiplying the preference rating by the weights and obtaining the resultant weighted score.
6) Summing up the weighted score for each location.

The location with the maximum point is desirable

8.8.2. *Location Break-even Analysis*

The procedure for location break-even analysis involves the following steps:

1) Determining all relevant costs that are associated with the locations.
2) Classifying the costs for each location into annual fixed costs and per unit variable costs
3) Plotting the costs associated with each location on a single chart of annual costs on Y axis versus annual volume on X axis.
4) Choosing the location with the lowest total costs at the expected production volume.

8.8.3. *Factors Affecting Location Decisions*

Selecting a facility location is influenced by various factors like geographical consideration, local laws & regulations, economic confederations, competition etc.

Table 8.1: Factors Affecting Location Decisions

Level	Factors	Considerations
Region /Country	Locations of raw materials or supplies, Location of market labour	Proximity, modes and costs of transportation, Quantity available/Proximity, distribution costs, target market, Trade practices/restrictions Availability [general and for specific skills], age distribution of work force, attitudes toward work, union or no union, productivity, wage scales, unemployment compensation laws.
Community	Facilities Services Attitudes Taxes Environmental regulations Utilities Development support	Schools, Churches, Shopping, Housing, Transportation, Entertainment, etc. Medical, Fire and Police Availability of Govt support through schemes and loans assistants , grants Tax concession and etc.
Site	Land Transportation Environmental/Legal	Cost, degree of development required, soil characteristics, room for expansion, drainage, parking Type ,roads, rail spurs, air freight and Zoning restrictions

8.9. Choice of Technology

The backbone of any small business is the products or services it offers and the most effective way to approach a small business is either by creating an unique product or service that would be of great demand or to adopt something that is currently available in the market.

The critical elements of a small business operating strategy are products and process that go together. The business environment is dynamic and pressures for change in product or service design can come from within the from within the firm, competitors, suppliers, legal sources and legislations. The relationship between the product selected and the organization structure can be seen by considering the technology by which the product is produced. The choice of product for new organizations determines the production technology.

Technology selection affects the management of human resources, plant and materials capacity of the operating system and also the external environment like competitors, markets and society. The technology chosen to produce product or service should be flexible to take care of the changes in their designs.

Technology is defined as a combination of labour, machines, processes, energy and other inputs directly involved in the transformation of materials into products. Technology increases the outputs of industrial and non-industrial sector. It improves the quality and reliably of the products and helps business units to save the capital costs. It creates new resources and a primary source of improving productivity. Technological consideration occurs at two levels.

1) General technological feasibility which can be thought of decision regarding the theoretical feasibility of making the product (Major choice of technology)

2) The general nature of processing system (Minor choice of technology), the specific equipment to be employed (specific component choice)

Considerations aiming at determining the most efficient relationship between processing steps (Sequential) are to be made. Firms using existing technology should continue interest in improving it as long as changes are desirable economically and can be justified. Reducing unit cost, increasing the rate of output and improving the yield are the motives for seeking improvements in existing technologies.

The various criteria for evaluating production process and equipment selection are:

1) Product/service requirements.
2) Technological feasibility.
3) Financial considerations.
4) Labour and skill requirements.
5) Output and capacity needs.
6) Compatibility with existing facilities.
7) Flexibility.
8) Raw material requirements.
9) Size and weight limits imposed by plant or building.
10) Maintainability.
11) Spare parts inventory requirements.

The selection of the most desirable technology can be aided by tools like capital investment analysis, economic analysis, linear programming models, marginal costing, breakeven analysis, and incremental analysis. Time study and Motion study, work measurement, work standards can be used as aids for integrating the human factors in process equation. The following are few process know how sources for small scale manufacturing units.

1) National Research and Development Corporation.

2) Council of Scientific and Industrial Research.

3) Research laboratories recognized by CSIR.

The following are institutions equipped with the facilities of pilot plan, prototype product manufacturing facilities, product testing, Research and Development of new products:

1) Industrial Research Laboratories set up by various State Governments.

2) Central Institute for Plastics Engineering and Training, Madras/Ahmedabad.

8.10. Forms of Business Organisation

An entrepreneur has various options that need to be understood before abruptly taking a decision to choose for one or the other form of ownership of business because, every form has its inherent advantages and disadvantages, limitations, attendant risks and manner of operation. Further, the decision about choosing a specific form of ownership is guided by various factors such as;

i. The entrepreneur's personal capacity to take decisions, manage and control particular situations.

ii. The entrepreneur's capacity to cover risk

iii. The entrepreneurs educational background, technical expertise and experience or expertise in manufacture of the proposed product and

iv. The entrepreneur's capacity to invest in the proposed unit.

Any business activity in order to be coordinated and managed needs to be organized in formal pattern of relationship relating to ownership and control. Entrepreneurs may opt any of the following forms of ownership, and, they are free to change the form of ownership chosen confining to these forms, whenever wanted.

1. Individual proprietorship

2. Partnership-Joint family business

3. Partnership with others

4. Private limited company

5. Public limited company

6. Co-operative society

1. Proprietorship

Proprietorship is a business owned & controlled by only one person. All assets in the firm are owned by the proprietor who sows, reaps and harvests the output of his labour. This form is one of the most popular forms in India and the reason is the advantages it offers.

In this form of ownership, business can be started simply after obtaining necessary manufacturing license and permits.

Advantages of Single Proprietorship are

i. Simplicity of organization.

ii. Owner's freedom to make all decisions.

iii. Owner's enjoyment of all profits.

iv. Minimum legal restrictions.

v. Ease of discontinuance.

vi. Tax advantage.

vii. Secrecy.

Disadvantages

1. Owners possible lack of ability and experience.

2. Limited opportunity for employees.

3. Difficulty in raising capital.

4. Limited life of the firm.

5. Limited size.

6. Unlimited liability of proprietor.

2. Partnership

It is defined as an association of two or more persons to carry on as co-owners of a business, for profit.

Partnership is preferred when the quantum of business is expected to be moderate and the entrepreneur desires that the risk involved in the operation be shared. In India, the law relating to the partnership is given in the Indian partnership Act, 1930. A partnership comes into existence when two or more persons agree to share the profits of a business, which they run together. This business may be carried on by all the persons or by any of them acing for all. Those, who thus enter into an agreement are individually called as 'partners' and collectively as 'firm'. The name under which their business is carried on is called the 'firm name'.

The characteristics of a partnership are:

(i) Partnership is the outcome of a voluntary agreement between the persons, who after the agreement has been arrived at, would be known as partners. A partnership agreement should have all the essentials of a valid contract.

(ii) Maximum number of members a firm may have is twenty (other than banking activities). A partnership becomes illegal if more than stipulated number of personal is included.

The followed details are spelled out in the partnership agreement:

1. The objective and duration of partnership
2. The duties and rights of partners
3. Method of dividing profits & losses of the business.
4. Procedure to be followed when any of the partner wishes to withdraw from the partnership or a new partner enters the business.
5. Manner of Settlement of controversies arising out of the agreement

(iii) The business may be carried on by all the partners or it may be carried on by any one of them acting for all.

The person of the group who managers the business do so as agent for all the partners is bound by their acts and liable to account for all.

(iv) The profits and losses of the business are shared equally by all the partners, unless specifically mentioned in the agreement.

Advantages of Partnership are

i.   Ease of organization
ii. Combined talent judgment and skill
iii. Increased sources of capital and credit
iv. Improved chances of growth
v.   Tax advantage

Disadvantages

i.   Unlimited liability
ii. Limited life
iii. Divided Authority
iv. Danger of Personal Disagreements

3. *Company*

Company is a form of ownership which is an association of persons in which money is contributed by them, to carry on some business or undertaking. Persons contributing the money are called the 'shareholders' or 'the members of the company'. The law relating to companies in India is contained in The Companies Act of 1956.

The Characteristics of a Company are

a) The company after incorporation, in the eyes of law is treated as a person (artificial person). The company may sue or be sued by its members/shareholders whenever any breach of their rights or duties is committed. As a person the company can enter into contracts in its own name and likewise may sue and be sued in its own name.

b) The company can neither think, no do anything by itself, although an independent person, and therefore, its affairs are managed by a Board of Directors, who manages the affairs of the company on behalf of the company and in accordance with its Memorandum and Articles of Association.

c) When any contract is entered in the name of the company, the company 'seal is required to be put on the same in order to make the contract binding on the company.

d) Being, a creation of law the company is not affected by the leaving, joining, death, insolvency or insanity of any of its shareholders. As the company comes into existence only through a process of law. It can only be dissolved through a process prescribed by law.

e) The shares of a joint Stock company other than private company are freely transferable.

f) The members have limited liability. In case of a company limited by share, the liability of the members of the company is limited to the nominal value of shares held by them, In case of a company limited by guarantee, members are liable only to the extent of the amount guaranteed by them.

Entrepreneurs may form either a private company or a public company depending upon the type of restriction they want to impose upon their organisation.

Under section 3(i) (iii) of the companies Act, a Private company has been defined as a company which by its Articles of Association

1. Restricts the right to transfer the shares, if any,

2. Limits the number of its members to fifty, and

3. Prohibits any invitation to the public to subscribe for the shares or the debentures of the company.

Under section 3(i) (iv), a public company is a company which is not private company. By implication, therefore, public company is one, registered under the Companies Act, which places no restriction by its Articles of Association on the transfer of shares or on the maximum number of members/shareholders and can invite the public to subscribe for its shares, debentures and public deposits.

Advantages of a Company

Some of the important advantages of a company are:

i. Limited liability.
ii. Perpetual existence.
iii. Transferability of shares.
iv. Expansion potential.
v. Representative management.

Disadvantages of a Company

i. Legalities of formation.
ii. Legal restrictions.
iii. Heavy Taxation.
iv. Lack of secrecy.

CHAPTER-IX

EXPORT AND INTERNATIONAL COOPERATION OF MSMEs

9.1. Introduction

Exporting supplies a customer in one country with products manufactured in another country. Exports constitute an essential part of any nation's economic activity. Export maximum possible to balance of payment deficits as quickly as possible. Export promotion is particularly important for developing countries, so that, they may obtain all their developmental requirements besides servicing their external debts.

9.2. Export Policy

The process of industrial development in India resulted in redefinition and expansion of the export sector in 70's. The Development of capabilities for export of capital goods, engineering goods, manufactured products, project and services, and also setting up joint individual ventures abroad are important outcomes of this products.

The term export policy refers to all the policies that have either direct or indirect bearing of the export of the country. The need for exports and the efforts to diversify India's export products have been the objective of the government since independence. However, it was only in **1970** the government formulated a positive policy. 'Export policy resolution **1970**'. This is considered as a land mark in the history of exports of India.

9.2.1. *Features of the Export Policy*

1) Government recognized that, in order to achieve national self-reliance and to reduce dependence on foreign countries, our export earnings to be expanded at a higher rate.

2) It great stress on the development and expansion of export- oriented industries as a means of study increase in export earnings.

3) It acknowledges that the country has high export potential in many areas and the adoption of appropriate policies and measures will help to achieve the objective. It also recognizes the need for keeping policies stable for reasonable period of time.

4) It lays stress on

    a) Consolidating the position in the export of traditional products and

    b) Identifying products having a long–term export potential with a view to adopting special measures and programmes for their development.

5) The need to evolve suitable policies and measures to encourage export-oriented industries.

6) To assist industry with a view to:
    a) Making their products competitive.
    b) Modernizing Machinery.
    c) Improving quality control.
    d) Providing aids.
    e) Providing adequate and timely sequence and
    f) Providing adequate shipping facilities at reasonable freight rates.

The new economic policies have been helpful in restoring India's credit worthiness in world markets and, foreign entrepreneurs and investors have realized the vast potential of India's domestic market and the scope for building up a large trade in export s to neighbouring countries. Many foreign entrepreneurs have already been implementation projects in the export processing zones and also in food processing industries. The objective of the government has also been to permit Indian and foreign entrepreneurs to enter power, telecommunications and even petroleum sectors so that the central state government can lay greater emphasis on the execution of social welfare programmes.

9.3. Export Scenario of MSMEs in India

Worldwide, the MSMEs have been accepted as the engine of economic growth for promoting equitable development. As per the available statistics (4th Census of MSME sector), this sector employs an estimated 59.7 million persons spread over 26.1 million enterprises in the country. It is estimated that in terms of value, MSME sector accounts for about 45% of the manufacturing output and around 40% of the total exports of the country. MSMEs play an important role in export promotion of the country. To maintain its niche in the international and global markets, MSMEs are required to remain globally competitive. They have to continuously update themselves to meet the challenges emerging out of changes in technology, changes in demands, emergence of new markets, etc.

Table 9.1: Export of the MSMEs in India

Distribution of Exporting Units in India					
S.No	Nature of Exports	Number of Units	Type of Enterprises	Percentage of Export	Location of exporting MSMEs	Distribution percentage
1	Direct Exporting	12821	Micro	85.83	Rural	31.58
2	Indirect Exporting	6352	Small	12.75	urban	68.42
3	Both	27502	Medium	01.42		
	All India total	46625		100		100

(Source: Final report of fourth Census of MSMEs registered sector -Government of India 2011-12 .Pp 65.)

In this connection, Uttar Pradesh, Tamil Nadu and Maharashtra are the three top level exporting state in India. Nearly fifty thousand numbers of MSMEs' units are exporting to our home made products to the various countries in this earth. Majority of MAMEs are exporting their goods from urban background with Micro level. (Table 9.1)

9.3.1. *Composition of Indian Exports*

The composition of imports and exports is an important aspect of a country's foreign trade. The types of goods imported and exported indicate the stage of development of economy, the standard of living of the people and the nature of economic activity in the country.

The exports from this country are classified as consumer goods, agriculture by-products and semi-processed goods. The consumer goods exported are tea, cotton cloth, black paper, kernels, tobacco, readymade garments etc. Among the raw materials and intermediate goods exported are jute, hides and skins, metallic ores, raw and waste cotton, vegetable oils and seeds. The 'others' include wool, lubricants, art silk, machinery and transport equipment. Tea, jute cotton and other traditional exports from this country still account for more than one-half of the export trade.

Coffee, tea, oil meals, tobacco, cashew nuts, spices raw cotton, rice accounted, **readymade** garments and leather products are the important export varieties in India. During the last two decades, the export items from India have been a considerable shift from traditional items to electronic goods, heavy engineering goods, plant and machinery, wrist watches sophisticated scientific instruments. India had made a foothold in developed markets like Europe and American markets.

Agriculture and allied products have been the major source of export growth. There are good scope for chemicals, drugs, paramedical and also product such as tea, coffee, cashew, spices & tobacco. Agro processed exports and food processing industry hold promise with proper packing, quality, and tie up arrangements with distribution chain in the developed countries.

9.4.   Export Promotion and International Cooperation

A developing economy usually needs large imports of capital goods, technology and even consumer goods to implement in development in programmes. Imports have to be paid for by exports. Therefore, large exports are essential for financing large imports. The main thrust of commercial policy of the government is to make the foreign trade sector serve the socio-economic goals of national development. The government of India has taken a number of measures to promote experts in the post liberalisation era as, assistance and assistance for export production. It has also sponsored a number of organisations to provide different types of assistance to the exporters.

In recent years, the MSME sector has consistently registered higher growth rate compared to the overall industrial sector. With its agility and dynamism, the sector has shown admirable innovativeness and adaptability to survive the recent economic downturn and recession. However, MSMEs have been facing great challenge in the era of globalization and liberalization. With its consistent growth performance and abundant high skilled manpower, India provides enormous opportunities for investment, both domestic and foreign. To exploit this potential, M/o MSME and its organizations, through its various Schemes and Programmes, are providing support to the Indian MSME sector by giving them exposure of the international market; foreign technology; sharing of experiences and best management practices in the international arena.

In continuation of this Endeavour, M/o MSME has entered into long term agreements, Memorandum of Understanding/Joint Action Plan with 17 countries viz., Tunisia, Romania, Rwanda, Mexico, Uzbekistan, Lesotho, Sri Lanka, Algeria, Sudan, Cote d'Ivoire, Egypt, Republic of South Korea, Mozambique, Botswana, Indonesia, Vietnam and Mauritius. Besides, different organizations under this Ministry have also been maintaining close interaction with their counterparts in the foreign countries for the development of Indian MSMEs. The National Small Industries Corporation (NSIC) Ltd., a public sector enterprise under this Ministry has entered into long term agreements with partner institutions/organizations in 24 different countries. In view of M/o MSME's long experience of over half a decade in the policy, programme and implementation of the schemes in the MSME sector, many of the developing economies of Asia and Africa seek guidance from it and/or its organizations. The organizations of the M/o MSME have provided consultancy services and also assisted in setting up of different projects, in the Afro-Asian countries

9.4.1. *International Cooperation Schemes*

International Cooperation (IC) Scheme, being implemented by the Ministry of Micro, Small and Medium Enterprises (MSME), is an ongoing Scheme of the Ninth Plan (under implementation since 1996), which has been continued for the Twelve Plan (2012-13 to 2016-17) with an outlay of Rs. 24.50 crore. For the Annual Plan 2013-14, a provision of Rs. 5.00 crore was earmarked. Technology infusion and/or up gradation of Indian micro, small and medium enterprises (MSMEs), their modernisation and promotion of their exports are the principal objective of assistance under the Scheme.(Annual Report of MSMEs, GOI ;2014-15)

1. Deputation of MSME business delegations to other countries for exploring new areas of technology infusion/up gradation, facilitating joint ventures, improving the market of MSMEs products, foreign collaborations, etc.

2. Participation by Indian MSMEs in international exhibitions, trade fairs and buyer-seller meets in foreign countries as well as in India, having international participation.

3. Holding international conferences and seminars on topics and themes of interest to the MSMEs.

4. Significant Meetings with Foreign Dignitaries and Delegations by Ministry of Micro, Small and Medium Enterprises and its organisations like O/o DC (MSME) and NSIC

9.5. Institutional Framework for Promotion of Exports

To carry out the task of export promotion effectively, India has developed a fairly elaborate institutional framework, to assist the export sector apart from the organisations which were established specifically for export promotion. They are:

1) Export Promotion Councils (EPCs)

2) The Trade Development Authority (TDA), New Delhi.

3) Indian Institute of Foreign Trade (IIFT), New Delhi.

4) Indian institute of Packaging (IIP)

5) Export Inspection Council (EIC)

6) Indian Council of Arbitration (ICA).

7) Marine Products Export Development Authority (MPEDA), Cochin.

8) Zonal Export-import advisory committee- functioning in New Delhi, Bombay, Calcutta& madras.

9) Federation of Indian Export Organizations. (FIEO), New Delhi.

10) Trade &Industry Organizations like the Chamber of Commerce & Industry.

11) State Trading Agencies like State trading Corporation (STC), Minerals & Metals Trading Corporation (MMTC).

1. *Ministry of Foreign Trade*

A new department of international Trade in the Ministry of commerce was set up early in 1962. A new high level board of trade was also constituted to review all aspects of trade and to advice the government of export promotion. The department was later converted into a full-fledged Ministry of foreign trade. The ministry prepares comprehensive export plans, fixes targets and lays down cost reduction programmes for principal export commodities. The Board undertakes detailed commodity-wise and country wise of India's exports.

An institution called the Indian Institute of foreign Trade has also set up as an autonomous organisation for carrying out programmes of training research and market studies.

2. *Export promotion Advisory Council*

The council, which consists of leaders of industry and trade and is presided over by the ministry of international Trade, has been set up as a forum to discuss adequacy and efficacy of the various export promotion measures. It reviews the general export policy of the Government every six years.

Regional Export Promotion Advisory Committees, consisting of businessmen, have been set up in Madras, Bombay, Cochin and Calcutta to make detailed studies of the export possibilities exported from various regions and advise the Government on specific problems of exports from the regions. The Council and Regional Committees make it possible to have close liaison to be maintained between the Government and the business community, and specific difficulties of individual exports are quickly resolved.

3. *Export Promotion Councils*

The EPCs are non-profit organisation registered under the Companies Act or the Societies Registration Act. As the case may be. They are supposed by financial assistance from the Central Government.

The main role of the EPCs is to project India's image abroad as a reliable supplier of high quality goods and services. In particular the EPCs shall encourage and monitor the observance of international standards and specification by exporters. The EPCs shall keep abreast of the trends and opportunity in international markets for goods and services and assist their members in taking advantage of such opportunities in order to expend, diversify exports.

At present, there are 19 Export Promotion Council (EPCs), whose basic objective is to promote and develop exports of the country. Each Council is responsible for the promotion of a particular group of products, project and services.

These have been set up for a number of important export commodities. their functions are to advice the Government, local authorities and public bodies on matters relating to the export of the commodities in question and take measures such as market surveys, trade delegations, exhibitions, publicity, quality control, etc., to promote exports of these commodities.

Moreover, Commodity Boards, have been set up for certain commodities, such as tea, coffee, coir, etc., functions of which are to promote the production and exports of these goods.

The major functions of the EPCs are as follow:

a) To provide commercially useful information and assistance to their members in developing and increasing their export;

b) To offer professional advice to their members in areas such as technology up gradation, quality and design improvement standards and specifications, product development, innovation etc.

c) To organize visits of delegation of its members abroad to explore overseas market opportunities, and

d) To organise participation in trade fairs, exhibitions and buyers-seller meets in India and abroad.

Any export/importer may apply to become a number of an EPC and such application shall be considered and disposed of within one month therefore, in accordance with the rules regulations of the EPC. On being admitted to membership, the applicant shall be granted forthwith a Registration-Cum-Membership Certificate (RCMC).

4. *Export Risks insurance Corporation and Export Credit and Guarantee Corporation*

The Export Risks Insurance Corporation was set up with the purposed of encouraging export. Its function was to provide insurance against risks involved in exports credit terms. The corporation covered commercial risks, such as protracted default by the buyer and his insolvency, and political risks, such as civil war, import control, exchange restrictions, etc. these risks were not insured by private insurance companies, and a public corporation for this purpose was essential. The corporation did useful service and made a large contribution to the promotion of exports.

In January 1964, the Export Credit and Guarantee Corporation were established, in which the Export Risks Insurance Corporation was merged. The purpose of the corporation is to strengthen and supplement the activities of the exciting export finance institutions. It provides export credit and guarantee and supplementary credit facilities, essential for promotion and development of exports.

5. *The State Trading Corporation*

The state Trading Corporation was set up in May **1956**. Its principal function is to enlarge the scope of exports from this country and to facilitate essential imports. The corporation enters into direct trade contracts and helps in concluding them between foreign and Indian traders. It guarantees quality of goods, observance of delivery schedules and payments on time, and thus, encourages trade in the directions. The Corporation helps in boosting up export of commodities falling within its purview.

In October **1963**, a separate Minerals and Trading Corporation was established was established to handle exports of minerals and metals. The corporation has been instrumental in simulating and increasing exports of these commodities.

6. *Export Development Authority*

This organisation was set up in September 1970, to assist enterprise to build up exports through a package of personalised services in the field of trade information, research and analysis, merchandising, and export production and promotion. It has since announced a packaging of services for its member units interested   in exporting selected goods, mainly engineering goods.

7. *Commodity Corporation*

A number of corporations of different commodities were set up in July 1970, such as the Cashew Corporation, the Cotton Corporation, the Jute Corporation, and the Projects and equipment Corporation. These corporations are playing now an important part of the institutional framework to promote exports.

8. *The Marine Products Development Authority*

The Authority is responsible for organisation, coordination, regulation and growth of the marine products export industry, with special reference to the quality of the material, processing, packaging storage, transport, marketing, and attendant investigations.

9. *Awards and certificates of merit are now given to firms for outstanding export performance*

9.6.   Export Promotion Schemes

A number of schemes are offered by the Central govt. to augment the export promotion in our nation. Prominent among them are:

a)   Export promotion capital goods scheme

b)   Duty exemption scheme

c)   Diamond gem and jewellery export promotion schemes

d)   Gold/Silver jewellery and articles export promotion schemes

a. *Export Promotion Capital Goods Scheme*

Capital goods may be imported with a licence under the EPCG scheme at a concessional rate of customs duty according to certain conditions, but subject to an export obligation to be fulfilled over a period of time. Such export obligation may be reckoned from the date of customs clearance of the first consignment of such imported goods.

A manufacture-exporter to be eligible to import capital goods under the scheme should have been a regular exporter for a period of not less than three years. However, import of capital goods under the scheme may also be allowed, on merits, to other manufacturer exporters who are new exporters or whose exporter export performance is for a period of less than three years. Testing equipment, R & D Equipment, packaging machinery and such other machinery or equipment as may be a specified may also be imported under the scheme. Both new and second hand capital goods may be imported the scheme.

The export obligation to be fulfilled by the importer shall be independent of any other obligation undertaken by the importer and shall be over and above the average level of exports made by him in the preceding three licensing years. Further, the export obligation under the scheme shall be in the form of direct exports of the products manufactured with the capital goods permitted to be imported. For the purpose, deemed exports and third party exports shall not be taken into account.

Import of capital goods under the scheme shall be subject to the Actual User condition. An application for grant of licence with the procedure specified in this behalf. A manufacturer-exporter shall be required to execute a bond with the licensing authority in the prescribed from supported by a bank guarantee for the value and period as mentioned in the licence. A person holding a licence under EPCG Scheme for import of capital goods may source the capital goods from a domestic supplier instead of importing it. In the event of a firm contract between the parties for such sourcing, the domestic supplier may apply for the import of components under this scheme at a concessional rate of customs duty of 15% of the CIF value of such components for the manufacture and supply of the said capital goods to the EPCG licence holder. The export obligation pertaining to the import of the capital goods shall, however, continue to be discharged by the EPCG licence holder.

b. Duty Emption Scheme

Under the Duty Exemption Scheme, imports of duty free raw materials, components, intermediates, consumable, parts, spares including mandatory spares and packing materials for the purpose of export production may be permitted by the competent authority under the five categories of licenses mentioned hereinafter.

c. *Advance License*

An advance licence is granted for the duty free import of raw materials, components, intermediate, consumables, parts, spares including mandatory spares and packing materials. Such licences shall be subject to the fulfilment of a time-bound export obligation and value addition as may apply for a value addition as maybe specified. Advance licences may be based on either value or quantity. An exporter may apply for a value based or quantity based advance licence.

d. *Advance Intermediate License*

An advance Intermediate Licence is granted for the duty free import of raw materials, components, intermediates, consumables, parts, spares and packing materials by the intermediate manufacturer for supply under an agreement to the ultimate exporter holding a licence under the Duty Exemption Scheme. The Intermediate Licence holder shall have an option either to supply to a licence holder under the Duty Exemption Scheme or export directly within a specified period and on satisfying the requirements of value addition. The quantitative norms applicable to Advance Licences shall also apply to Advance Intermediate Licence. A special imprested licence is granted for the duty free import of raw materials, components, intermediates consumables, parts, spares including mandatory spares and packing materials to main/sub contractors for the manufacture and supply of products.

Export may apply for duty free licence, except special Imprested Licence, without an export order. In the case of an application without an export order, the value of the licence may not exceed the average of the FOB Value of exports of the applicant during the preceding three licensing years. Manufacture and merchants having an average annual turn-over of Rs.5 crores or more during the preceding three licensing years may apply for duty free licences, except Special imprested licence, to meet their needs of export production, without an export order the value of the licence may not exceed 25% of the said average annual turnover.

9.6.1. *Deemed Exports*

"Deemed exports" means those transaction in which the goods supplied do not leave the country rupees, but the supplies earn or save foreign exchange for the country.

Deemed exports shall be eligible for following benefits in respect of manufacture and supply of goods qualifying as deemed exports:

a. Duty exemption scheme under chapter VII

b. Duty drawback scheme.

c. Refund of terminal Excise duty.

d. Special import licenses, for such value of bearing such proportion to the value of the deemed exports, for the import of such items included in the Negative list import as may be specified under a scheme to be notified in this behalf.

It is the policy of the Central Government to encourage the manufacturers and exporters to attain internationally accepted standards of quality of their products. The Central Government will extend support and assistance to trade and industry associations to launch nationwide programme on quality awareness and promote the concept of total quality management.

The Central Government. Has introduced, a scheme to recognize and suitably reward manufactured who have acquired the ISO 9000 (series) or the BIS 14000 (series) or any other internationally recognized equivalent certification of quality. Such manufacturers will be eligible for grand of special import licences, for such value of bearing such proportion to the value of their exports, for the import of such items included in the Negative List of Imports as may be specified under the scheme to be notified in this behalf.

9.7. Financial Institutions

There are financial and insurance institutions which provide financial insurance and related assistance to the export sector. The Export-Import (EXIM) Bank, Export Credit Guarantee Corporation of India Limited (ECGC), the General Insurance Companies, are all playing a very important role in this area.

9.7.1. *Export -Import Bank of India*

Export-Import Bank of India (Exim Bank) is a public sector financial institution created by an Act of Parliament, the Export and Import Bank of India Act, 1981. Exim Bank was set up for the purpose of financing, facilitating and promoting foreign trade of India.

Exim Bank is the principle financing institution for coordinating the working of institutions engaged in financing export and import trade of India. The Exim Bank is to finance India Exports that leads to continuity of foreign exchange for India.

The Bank came into existence January 1982 and commenced operations from March 1, 1982.

Operation

The present focus of Exim Bank is on export finance. The Bank finances export of Indian machinery, manufactured goods, and consultancy and technology services on differed payment terms. Exim Bank finance is also available for export production stages. Exim Bank undertakes co-financing with global and regional development and assist Indian exporters in their efforts to participate in such overseas projects.

Services

Exim Bank's advisory services provide access to Euro financing and global credit for Indian companies engaged in exports. The Bank workers closely with Indian companies in designing financing packages for export-oriented industries in India, overseas joint ventures and projects

a. Financing Programmes

Deferred Payment Exports

Term finance is provided to Indian exporters of eligible goods and services which enable them to offer deferred credit to overseas buyers. Deferred credit can also cover Indian consultancy, technology and other services. Commercial banks participate in this programme directly under risk syndication arrangements.

Pre-shipment Credit

Finance is available from Exim bank for companies executing export contracts involving cycle time exceeding six months. The facility also enables provision of rupee mobilization expenses for construction/turnkey project exporters.

Term loans for Export Production

Exim Bank provides term loans to export oriented units, in free trade zones and computer software exporters.

Overseas Investments Finance

Indian companies establishing joint ventures are provided finance towards their equity contribution in the joint venture.

Finance for Exporting Marketing

This programme which is a component of a World Bank Loan, helps exporters implement their export market development plans.

b. Loans to Foreign Governments, Companies and Financial Institutions

Overseas Buyer's Credit

Credit is directly offered to foreign entities for import of eligible goods and related services, on deferred payment.

Lines of Credit

Beside foreign governments, finance is available to foreign financial institution and government agencies to on-lend in the respective country for import of goods and services from India.

Relending Facility to Banks Overseas

Relending facility is extended to banks overseas to enable them to provide term finance to their clients world-wide for imports from India.

c. Loans to Commercial Banks in India

Export Bills Rediscounting

Commercial banks in India who are authorized to deal in foreign exchange can rediscount their short term export bills with Exim Bank, for usance periods.

Refinance of Export Credit

Authorized dealers in foreign exchange can obtain from Exim Bank 100% refinance of post shipment credits extended to India exporters for eligible Indian goods.

Guaranteeing of Obligations

Exim Bank participates with commercial banks in India in the issue of guarantees required by Indian Companies for export contracts and for execution of overseas construction and turnkey projects.

Exim Banks is fully owned by the government of India and is managed by a Board of Directors with representation from Government, financial institutions, banks business community. The operations are grouped into project Finance, Trade Finance, Overseas Investment Finance supported by planning and Co-ordination Groups.

9.7.2. The Export Credit and Guarantee Corporation Limited

This is an autonomous body, functioning under the guidance and supervision of the Ministry of Foreign Trade. This corporation provides the cover in various forms against different types of financial assistance given by the banks. It functions under the administrative control of the ministry of commerce and its functions are:

1) To provide a range of credit risk insurance covers to exporters against losses in the export of goods and services;

2) To provide production investment;

3) To offer guarantees to banks and financial institutions to enable exporters to obtain better facilities from them ;and

4) To provide insurance cover against fluctuations in exchange rates.

    The various covers issued by the ECGC may be divided broadly into following four groups viz.

    a) Standard policies

    b) Specific polices

    c) Financial Guarantees and

a. Special Scheme for SSI's

With a view to enabling the small scale sector to participate to greater extent in the export activities of the country, ECGC provides special facilities to small scale exporters by offering high percentage of risk cover, and procedural relaxations under its policies and guarantees.

These facilities will apply to exporters whose annual export turnover is not more than Rs.25 lakhs shall be deemed to be small scale exporters, irrespective of their total business turnover.

Further, exports made by qualifying small scale exports through:

a) Co-operative of artisans.

b) Co-operatives or associations of consortia of small scale industries.

c) State small scale industries corporation and

d) National small industries corporation are also eligible for these special facilities.

b. *Main Facilities Provided Under the Scheme are*

Higher cover of 90% for banks under the whole turnover packing credit guarantees and higher cover of 90% under whole turnover post-shipment Export credit guarantee in respect of exporters who have taken ECGC contracts/shipment policy, and 65% cover for non-policy holders. Cover under standard policy is increased to 95% against commercial risk and exceed Rs.5 lakhs. The waiting period for payment of all types of claims is reduced to half the normal stipulated period.

The ECGC has also evolved a simplified scheme with the objective of helping small exporters viz, the 'Lumpsum premium scheme'. The scheme is applicable to the exporters whose annual export turnover does not exceed Rs.10 lakhs. The maximum liability of policy under the scheme is restricted to Rs.5 lakhs. The rate of premium on the policy is 50 paise per Rs.100/- per annum on the maximum liability of the policy, payable as a Lump sum to observe all the terms & conditions of the policy but they are not required to submit monthly shipment declarations.

9.8.   Facilities to Small Exporters

Government has taken a number of measures to enlarge the production base, to help improve the productive efficiency and to make the products more cost competitive. Measures in these directions include supply of raw materials and other inputs, facilities to establish and expand productive capacity, facilities for organisation of better technology etc.

A number of steps have been taken to assist the exporter in their marketing efforts. These include conducting, sponsoring of , otherwise assisting in market surveys and research collection, storage, dissemination of marketing information, organising and facilitating participation in international trade fairs and exhibitions, credit facilities, release of foreign exchange for export marketing activities, assistance in export procedures, provision of insurance cover for export risks, quality control and pre-shipment inspection, identifying markets and products with export potential, helping buyer-seller interaction etc.

The marketing development fund established in 193-64 is intended to be utilized to develop export market for Indian goods. Expenditure incurred on certain market development programmes are refunded either wholly or partially from this fund.

Trade exhibitions are held abroad and export SSI units are given opportunity and assistance in exhibiting their selected items in these exhibitions. The Small Industries Development Organisation (SIDO) provides assistance towards handing, clearing insurance, publicity, lenient etc. without recovering this expenditure from the participants.

The trade enquires generated in these exhibitions are circulated the trade delegations and sales-cum-study team are sponsored from the small scale sector under MDA scheme of the ministry of finance which provides reimbursement of 60% of the expenditure, in addition to participations/commodity fairs held in various parts of the country through the field organisations in collaboration with other concerned organisations.

The government of India has been making radical reforms in the sphere of import and export trade since July, 1991. The new stable Export-import policy (1992-97), which is amended once in a quarter has removed unnecessary controls and restriction on trade. Except, for limited number of items of items specified in the negative list, all experts and imports have been freed from bureaucratic controls.

The Expert-import Policy allows various exports/imports entitlements to exporting units under the various schemes covered under the policy. These schemes primarily relate to advance licensing scheme, imports under Indo-Us MOU, scheme of 100% EOUs, setting up of units in Free Trade Zones/Export Processing Zones. The proposals received from SSI units are considered by the government and recommended for granting of various licence entitlements to the importers to help them to meet their requirements of materials etc. Imports under some of the schemes are allowed without payment of customs duty. The Export import policy provides for double weight age on exports from small scale units for recognition as Export/Trading house.

The new policy contains a number of new incentives for generation of exports. Duty free imports relating to exports production have been liberalized and import duty on capital goods reduced with increased export obligation. While deemed exports have been accorded favourable treatment, the policy has virtually eliminated canalization of imports. Except for some petroleum products, edible oils, fertilizers and cereals, all other items have been de-canalised.

1) In the case of exports, 16 items have been de-canalised and these include castor oil, polythene, coal and coke, color picture tubes and sub assembles of TVs containing color tubes, rectified spirit, exposed cinematographic films. Video type cinema films, khandasari molasses, bimetal ore (black iron ore) with manages contents, railway passenger coaches and locomotives, raw Jute cuttings, sugar, iron ore, etc.,

2) The Government has decided to continue its support for the development of export houses and trading houses as instruments of promoting exports. Trading houses with 51% foreign equity for promoting exports have been made eligible for all benefits available to domestic exports and trading houses in consonance with the Export-Import policy. Established exports are allowed to open foreign currency accounts in approved banks.

3) To encourage exporters to set up EOUs and EPZ units, the net foreign exchange earned by EOUs and by EOUs and EPZ units are allowed to club it with the earnings of their parent/associated companies in the Domestic Tariff Area (DTA) for according export house, trading house, trading house or trading house status for the latter.

4) As state governments have a major role to play in achieving objective of enhanced export, they have been asked by the centre to exempt exports from all fiscal levies in order to ensure that exporters are capable of competing effectivity in the world markets.

5) The Union Budget 1995 reduced peak rate of import duty from 65% to 40% along with a package measures to reduce input costs for the capital goods sector, a series of special financing schemes for small scale and tiny, khadi & village industries and hike in the excise exemption limit for such units.

6) A new scheme has been proposed by the government under which the banking system will provide Rs.1000 crores on consortium basis to khadi village industry commission (KVIC). The KVIC will lend to viable units either directly or through state level boards and the loans from commercial banks will be generated by central and state governments.

7) A 7 point action plan has been formulated in consultation with banks to improve the flow of credit to SSI sector. Another feature is the setting up of specialized bank branches for small Industries in 85 identified districts each with more than 2000 registered SSI units.

8) To promote export capabilities of SSI units a Technology Development & Modernization Fund has also been established in the SIDBI to provide financial assistance to quality projects aimed at strengthening export capability of small industries.

9) Commerce Ministry operates MDA (Market Development Assistance) programme for export housing for subsidizing overseas trips & participation in trade fairs abroad by Indian entrepreneurs. The application has to be forwarded through Federation of Indian Export   Organizations (FIEO) Delhi. Under MDA, partial assistance is given as per prescribed guidelines towards air fare for sale/market study tours abroad, daily allowance, opening of foreign office/ware house, etc. it is open to exporters having trading house/star trading house, manufacturer etc.

9.9.   Issues in Exports

Though the small scale sector is making significant contribution to total exports, both direct & indirect, a large potential remains to be tapped. Indian's exports during the twenty-five years have shown a mixed trend. In more recent times importance of exports is being viewed not merely from the point of view of financing necessary imports and balance of payments, but also from the point of view of bringing out a qualitative transformation of the industry as well as the economy. The idea is that yardstick for the purpose. Exports are now recognized as engine for growth and imports as fuel for purpose of exports growth. It is in this sense that the importance of foreign trade sector increased significantly in the economy.

The rate of growth of India's exports has been rather slow as compared to the rate of growth of world exports, mainly owing to:

i.   Inadequate exportable surpluses.

ii.   Problem of quality control.

iii.   Competitive ability of rival producers.

iv.   Inadequate transportation and shipping facilities.

v.   India's exports, like exports from other developing countries are pitted against many tariff and non-tariff barriers imposed by the developed countries.

vi.   Lastly as per a World Bank report, it is contended that India's policy environment remains highly protectionist, interventionist and full of restrictive rules and in face of which exports require numerous off-setting arrangements.

With the increasing competition in international trade, small exporters have to compete in quality, price, delivery schedule, service, payment terms etc. with the onslaught of globalization of India's economy and the signing of **GATT** accord, the small exporters will have to compete with multinational giants in quality, packaging, Countries, inadequate availability of ISO **9000** certification for exporting to European Countries, inadequate availability of credit, need for modernisation (for example, textile industry), creation brand image (example leather garments) etc., are considered as problem areas for this sector

Chapter-X

Problems, Issues and Industrial Sickness in MSMEs

10.1. Introduction

While the small scale and cottage industries in India have been envisaged to play an important role in providing large scale employment opportunities at lower capital cost, establishment of wide entrepreneurial base ,dispersal of industries in rural and backward areas equitable distribution of national income and wealth through integration with   large industries, they are suffering from several problems and difficulties in connection with financial resources, marketing facilities, procurements of raw materials, effective techniques of manufacture etc.

10.2. Management Problems

Numerous small businesses suffer from underlying weaknesses which lead to mistakes that can adversely affect their return on investment. These management problems tend to arise when the business is expanded beyond the limits, a particular manager can cope with. The areas of weakness in small businesses that are management centred, carrying trouble are:

a. *Growth for Growth's Sake*

The most common of trouble is the widely held belief that the only road to success and the solution to all problems is growth of sales. Growth is not synonymous with capitalistic success. Infect, shrinking the number of products or product lines is usually the surest route to better profit and higher return on investment.

The mania for growth is commonly expressed in the battle to increase sales. Standard methods of accounting tend to encourage the belief that, higher profits automatically follow from higher sales. Several standard accounting techniques tend to mislead those who accept standard cost allocation as gospel

b. *Inadequate Cost Analysis*

Inadequate product-cost analysis blinds managers to the losses incurred by adding new products willy-nilly. Usually, there are one or more products or product lines that should be dropped.

Table 10.1: Major Incipient Problems of MSMEs in India

Sl no	Major Problems	Percentage
1	Lack of demand	41.94
2	Shortage of working capital	20.49
3	Non –availability of working capital	5.11
4	Power shortage	5.71
5	Labour problem	5.64
6	Marketing problem	11.48
7	Equipment problem	3.17
8	Management problem	6.46
	Total	100

(*Source: Final report of fourth Census of MSMEs registered sector -Government of India 2011-12 .Pp 53.*)

c. *lack of Balance Sheet Concern*

Another common failing is gearing the operations to the income statement and ignoring the balance sheet. Lack of concern with cash flow and the productivity of capital employed can be fatal to the small company that is on its own. Managers tend to seek new funds instead of making better use of those they already have.

Management deficiencies among small scale enterprises exist on several counts. Most of the small entrepreneurs undertake all the managerial functions by themselves primarily because they could not affords to employ managerial personal.. Secondly, the routine matters leading to virtually crisis management leaves little time and scope for organising objective decisions making.

Many a small entrepreneur does not seek proper guidance, information and counselling for decision making. Training of personnel is not considered as an important tool for up gradation. Entrepreneurial spirit to set up a new unit does exist but, innovativeness ant using unconventional tools in managing the enterprise are found lacking.

A long term perspective is found missing and tendency to for short term gains seem to cost seems growth and sustained profitability. Planning as a tool to organise oneself and manage resources is paid scant attention.

10.3. Financial Problems &Issues

Finance has been the foremost problems faced by the MSMEs enterprises. The problems are finance for the purchase and stocking materials, finance for holding finished products till they are sold out and finance paying wages. MSMEs producers are very poor who have little to offer as security. So, they have to depend on money lenders for finance and at times they have to make 'Distress Sales'.

The small scale industries need term capital to upgrade and modernize across the industries and different size groups in order to expand. It is reported that adequate institutional finance through term loans are not available to finance the same. One of the major impediments in getting adequate finance from the banks and financial institutions is due to the lack of trained personnel..

A severe credit squeeze can at times put sincere management in an awkward situation of managing recover. Many units get into further financial problems by borrowings from outside at exorbitant interest rates to tide over minimum financial needs.

Financial Management Issues

Entrepreneurs of small scale enterprises though start well, somewhere, in their day to day operations embrace failures. The reasons identified mostly are attributed to the financial mismanagement. Entrepreneurs are put up in a situation, wherein, they have a feeling of a well being but, the consolidation of accounts in the year end may indicate a disastrous situation, loss or almost being on the verge of losing. Sometimes, opportunities may come but, they cannot utilise. The reasons for such inadequacies are, inadequacy of funds & rigidity on the part of their bankers. Most often, the banker's don't cooperative due to entrepreneur's inability to maintain accounts and his inability to present his case strongly. All such problems can be overcome successfully if the entrepreneur pays some attention to financial management issues.

1) Entrepreneurs need to realize that the surest test of their business success is sufficient and growing profits i.e., profits that are growing from year to year. They have to determine the need for profit as well as lack of sufficient case at the right time may compel a fundamentally sound business to fail.

The sound of a business can be measured through breakeven analysis and the cash needs estimated through cash flow analysis. These analyses should be employed as poor planning tools to determine and ensure sound business health.

The Profit & loss account should be prepared more frequently to measure the success of day-to-day operation of the business and timely corrective action should be taken in case there is a loss.

2) The performance of various business activities relating output to input need to be measured by establishing performance standard to have a firm sense of direction, only then the business unit can be evaluated regularly and periodically followed by suitable corrective action to ensure smooth running of the business.

3) The accounting principle of conservation is to be adopted in situations of, uncertainty, in situations where a clear-cut decision is not possible, more often issue relating to valuation, timing etc. this principle would save entrepreneurs from awkward situations to save the face of entrepreneurs and their reputation. It would also add intense strength to the financial position and condition of the business.

4) The associated costs of funds raised and invested in various assets of the business need to be taken care of, as it the cost goes up profits will come down leading to decline of the return on investment. Therefore, analysis and supervision is required at the pre-investment stage i.e., after the assets have been purchased. To maximum utilization of each and every assets. More commonly pitfalls management aspects of assets like land and building, trade debts, (= bills receivable) cash etc. These pitfalls have to be avoided by the entrepreneur.

The measurement of receivables has always been a contentious issue in small scale units. Small scale entrepreneurs do not usually like to write off bad debts(uncollectible accounts) and reduce these from the balance sheet as well the income statements lest this reduce profits. In order to impress bankers and other creditors they prefer to carry on trade debts even after years of commencement of their business. Such practice needs to be eliminated.

Around the financial year end, entrepreneurs increase the trade debts unusually high so as to show an increased sales in a bid to impress their bankers. Such a practice is not only undesirable but can be dangerous and costly.

As a general rule, mainly when business is good, credit period should be reduced and business is dull, credit on sales may be extended. It may sound simple but would not be so easy in actual practice.

5) Cash, as a necessary evil acts as a lubricant that facilitates day-to-day operations. Cash is a use of funds as it appears on the assets side of the balance sheet. Whatever cash one is having whether in hand or in bank, comes from funds which are liabilities. Carrying too much cash increase cost of funds and carrying too less would mean facing embarrassment in business owing to inability to making to make payment of expenses due. One must carry the right amount of cash which would be an amount just sufficient to enable him/her make payment of all expenses as and when they fall due.

6) Good financial management is one which ensures that a business enterprise is live and kicking. That means the enterprise is growing. Business growth is dependent on solvency, credibility, ability to raise funds, availability of resources and liquidity.

Solvency is the ability of the business firm to pay off all debts which is measured by tangible net worth (= own funds or net worth-intangible assets). Solvency must be maintained at all times to keep the business running.

Credibility is the bedrock on which all business whether small, medium or large run. Maintaining credibility in business ensures sustainability and growth. Credibility ensures availability of adequate finance that leads to business viability. Credibility has to be established by the entrepreneurs which ensures finance, reputation and hence business growth.

A business enterprise using borrowed capital along with its own capital is said to be "Trading on equity". If equity is more than borrowed capital, it is described as, "Highly generated". Trading on equity should be kept within healthy limit. Entrepreneurs have to hold on their debt-equity ratio and should not allow it to worsen even if attractive opportunities are before them.

While insolvency is faced only once in the life of a business, liquidity is a short term solvency. Liquidity of a firm is its ability to meet expenses incurred in the short run. This is most essential for maintaining the firm's credibility and potential growth.

To tide over liquidity crunch, the entrepreneur should prepare projected cash flow statements on a monthly basis & take corrective action well in time.

7) For a comprehensive management of finance of a business enterprise both assets and liabilities are required to be managed. Managing liabilities is as important as assets management. Many a firm is known not to have progressed well because it could not manage its accrued expenses or trade credits.

The accrued expenses are those expenses like rent, salaries and wages etc. that get accrued but are not payable. These are important sources of funds. When an enterprise required funds, the entrepreneurs should not pay off the expenses till they become payable. Payment can be withheld till mutually & legally acceptable due dates and such funds can be utilised for day-to-day operations. At the same time, care must be taken to see that on the due dates sufficient funds are available to make payments and maintain business credibility.

The use of credit from suppliers is also an important source of meeting short-term requirements of funds. Entrepreneurs can utalise this facility without losing supplier's good will or compromising on other trade terms.

8) Most small business firms do not maintain accounts. In the absence of proper accounts, losses are incurred, pilferage take place: dues remain uncollected and most operations are conducted in the most unbusiness like manner. Survival and success of a small business depends on a healthy relationship between the three players, i.e. the bankers, the entrepreneur and the accountant. If an entrepreneur can't afford to appoint a full-time accountant, he should a employ a part-time accountant or maintain accounts himself. All successful businessmen realise that in the absence of adequate book-keeping and account they do not have correct picture of costs expenses, sales, trade, debts credits, tax liabilities, profits and return. It helps in establishing credibility with bankers, tax authorities and others. Every businessman must regularly maintain proper accounts to ensure financial planning corrective action and profits.

10.4. Marketing Problems & Issues

Marketing is the biggest problems affecting SSI performance. Beside finance , marketing is the key element that explains the closure of mall scale industrial units . in the initial stages of settings up units, many an entrepreneur do not choose the right product partly due to lack of proper information guidance and partly due to the bandwagon approach followed by potential entrepreneurs. This leads to marketing problems affecting the health of enterprise.

Small units produce low priced products compared to large scale units and as such are within the reach masses. However, the quality and reliability of SSI products is perceived by customers to be generally unsatisfactory, though small scale enterprises themselves do not acknowledge it. Most of the small units do not posses any quality mark for their products that reflects on their complacency and lack of entrepreneurial spirit for growth. Those units which produce quality products are unable to expose their quality tag due to the heavy promotional expenditures.

There is more intense intra-se competition within the small scale enterprises than with large scale enterprises. When compared to large scale enterprises, small scale enterprises are poor in all the competitive marketing attributes like. packaging, branding, distribution, promotion and after sales service .when direct competition, small scale enterprises are helped by their low prices. They are relying mostly provision of credit.

The costly handicrafts like Kashmiri Shawls and Banaras silk could not find markets because of the elimination of princes and Zamindars. Even in the available market, the products do not get their price due to the operation of middlemen. Further, the cottage industries are faced with the problem of costly transport and power supply in some cases.

Simply speaking, all marketing problems the small scale industries face are related to the 4 P's of marketing mix i.e. product, price, place and promotion.

Entrepreneurs need to understand the meaning and importance of marketing orientation and the need market assessment. Marketing orientation will help them to offer those products or services to the market that would satisfy some needs wants of the customers. The exercise of market assessment will help in understanding the nature and extent of demand, the competitive situation and prevailing trade practices.

The identification of target market segments helps an entrepreneur in turning the marketing efforts to the requirements of the customers, and in reducing wastages. Decisions on the efforts mix viz product, price, place & promotion and searching for a well-knit mix that has good consistency within its elements should be the major concerns to entrepreneur.

10.5. Operational Management Problems and Issues

Production management has traditionally been associated with manufacturing. Today it encompasses a large variety of other activities concerned with the conversion of inputs into outputs using physical resources so as to provide the defined utility/utilities to the customer while meeting the organizational needs of effectiveness, viability and quality.

Almost all units in small scale sector carry on production with outdated and obsolete implements and the method of production is also much antiquated. They do not have the facilities of researches and training to increase the output with modernized equipment. There are some institutions like All India Spinners Association, Khadi and Village Industries Development Board which attempt to impart to training to workers to improve the quality of production. Small Industries Service Institutes, to some extent, have removed the handicaps of small scale industries.

Most of the small-scale industries depend on large scale industries for the raw, materials. The handloom industry is wholly dependent on the supply of yarn from cotton mills. In the absence of proper organisation chennelising the flow of materials from the large scale sector, the cost of raw materials becomes very high and the artisans have to depend on middle-man who take away the cream of the credit.

The level of technology used by most entrepreneurs is rather poor and achievements with regard to several programmes launched by the government for its upgradation are moderate. Some units, with their process of manufacturing being manual produce poor quality products which in turn affect the image of the small scale sector and most of the smaller units cannot afford testing facilities. Some of the important operational management issues that need that need special attention are:

1) Entrepreneurs should be concerned with increased productivity i.e. achieving higher levels of output at the least cost of inputs. Products selection, the key strategic decisions of any organization which commits itself to the attempt to match the changes in environment, technology and consumer requirements while finalizing the design.

2) "Prototypes" are generally the handmade models which concretize the product formulation ideas. These prototypes need to be developed and thoroughly evaluated. Small entrepreneurs can avail the service of NSIC which has regional prototype Development Training/Testing centers.

3) Location of plant is a strategic decision that has to be arrived at after careful deliberations of various factors involved. It is a onetime decision and cannot be retracted without paying heavy penalties. Decisions will have to be taken based upon the following consideration:

    i.   Proximity to market.

    ii.   Nearness to raw materials.

    iii.   Adequate power and water arrangements and other infrastructural facilities.

    iv.   Transportation facilities and their costs.

    v.   Labour and wages,

    vi.   Laws and wages.

    vii.   Incentives, Land costs, Subsidies, backward areas

    viii.   Climate

    ix.   Ecology and environmental factors.

    x.   Political conditions.

4) Plant layout is an analytical and economic arrangement of various facilities like workmen, machines, equipment, materials ,plant services, incoming and outgoing materials, tools and intermediate storage and inspection areas with a view to achieve their maximum utilization, the facilities layout is a strategic decision since a layout once implemented cannot be changed easily. Some of the advantages of a good layout are:

    i.   Higher productivity.

    ii.   Economic utilization of floor space and other operating areas such as loading & unloading.

    iii.   Better supervision and control.

    iv.   Better working environment, and employee safety.

    v.   Minimum material handling.

    vi.   Lower investment in plant and building with better maintenance facility.

5) Production and operation management study will be complete only with the knowledge of industrial engineering, commonly called, "work study" which is a generic term for those techniques particularly, 'method study' and 'work measurement' which are used in the examination of human work in all its contests. Industrial engineering has gained importance throughout the world. It tells the entrepreneur the way to improve productivity.

6) Production planning and control is an effort to optimize the process of conversion of raw material into finished goods. This has to be an integrated function to derive maximum benefits of planning. It must be realised that the procurement and inspection of raw materials, the inventory levels of in process and finished goods, quality control, plant maintenance, production costs, manpower and training and the machinery equipment all have their influence on the planning of production operations.

7) Quality implementation should be treated as a total organizational effort. As a strategic decision, it is the responsibility of all functional mangers viz., purchase, production, warehousing (storage) and the transportation and packaging.

10.6. HRD Problems

MSMEs industries find it difficult to identify recruit and retain skilled technical and managerial personnel. They employ fresh hands; train them on the job to become skilled workmen. Many a small scale unit a significant number of workers, once they gain skills, leave them for greener pastures.

Though industrial relations in MSM enterprises are generally cordial, high turnover of the labour and absenteeism are two points of concern for entrepreneurs. This is attributed to lower wages being paid in the small scale sector.

To upgrade technical and management skills, in-service training is not being sought. Most of them depend on the job experience which includes the entrepreneurs themselves.

10.7. Industrial Sickness in MSMEs

10.7.1. Industrial Sickness

A sick unit is that which has incurred a cash loss for one year and is likely to continue incurring losses for the current year as well as in the following year and the unit has an imbalance in its financial structure such as current ratio is less than 1;1 and there is worsening of debt: equity ratio.

There are various reasons/causes for industrial sickness. They are:

i.   Internal and

ii.   External factors.

The internal factors mainly relate to poor quality of top management that may take several forms:

a) Excessive complacency growth mania
b) Poor financial control
c) Excessive centralization & authoritarianism
d) Weak board & a weak dog function
e) Excessive commitments to policies,
f) Poor financial or marketing management etc.(all constitute excessive conservatism)

The External Causes are Classified into

a) Industry specific factors related to stagnation or recession in the industry, competition faced by the unit, excess capacity in the industry etc.
b) Government related factors which include tax burden on the unit, legal restrictions on the unit, frequent changes in government policies etc.
c) Financial institutions based factors that include harness in dealing with the unit, delay in providing finance to the unit, inadequate working 7 or long term capital provided by them, their inexpert assessment of the client's project finance proposal etc.
d) Other factors like customer resistance to the unit's product, erratic availability of raw materials, components, power/fuel to the unit, inadequate transport facilities to the units etc.

10.7.2. Sickness in MSMEs in India

Industrial sickness is a natural concomitant of market economy. It is a complex and retrograde phenomenon. It blocks capital, impedes utilization of installed capacity, result in unemployment and regards to industrial growth. The Socio-economic implication of industrial sickness is rather serious.

Table 10.2: Distribution of Sick Units in MSMEs Registered Sector in India

Nature of Sickness	Total number of sick units			
	Micro	small	Medium	total
Loan outstanding	102322	13569	581	116472
Incipient sick	57710	2686	150	60556

Source; Final report of fourth Census of MSMEs registered sector-Government of India 2011-12 .Pp 52)

In terms of number stick units, West Bengal topped the list; in terms of amount frozen in such units, Maharashtra topped the list.

Sickness is caused by a number of internal and external factors. More often, a MSMEs unit get into vicious circle of sickness by a combination of factors.

MSMEs Industry is basically a "one man show" and therefore, in a disadvantageous position viz-a-viz a large industry which has separate departments with qualified manpower to manage affairs. Therefore, an average small entrepreneur has a high probability of committing errors; unfortunately in SSI sector, with very low equity base, the buoyancy is so less that, the whole project sinks as the result of even minor errors.

Mostly, sickness creeps into a SSI unit gradually; it needs to be identified at incipient state itself and tackled effectively. Before a unit becomes sick, it starts emanating early warning signals of impending sickness, which need to be taken cognizance of by both banker as well as entrepreneur. unfortunately, due to the peculiar problem" truancy of the pyramid" faced by MSMEs entrepreneurs, these small accounts are not effectively monitored by banks. The problem of sickness gets compounded by the entrepreneurs due to their shyness to discuss the problems with bankers invariably due to scepticism or fear.

Apart from the problem of payment from bigger industries, there is mismanagement of funds or non-management of as a whole, delayed recognition of sickness in time, delayed payments to suppliers etc. contribute to the sickness in small scale industries.

The Rehabilitation of Sick Micro, Small and Medium Enterprises envisages assistance for conducting a diagnostic study of sick enterprises, scrutiny of the above study report by a sub-committee of the State Level Inter-Institutional Committee (SLIIC) constituted by the Reserve Bank of India and chaired by the Secretary, Micro, Small and Medium Enterprises Department for rendering rehabilitation assistance to sick Micro, Small and Medium enterprises, which meets on every quarter. The Reserve Bank of India conducts the study on viability of sick units and the Banks provide financial assistance wherever possible along with other hand-holding steps like counselling the borrowers, analyzing the problems faced by the units etc. The Government have constituted the State Level Rehabilitation Committee (SLRC) under the Chairmanship of the Secretary to Government, Micro, Small and Medium Enterprises Department to look into the problems and the extent of sickness of MSMEs so as to suggest measures for their rehabilitation. The above Committee has to meet on quarterly basis to review and monitor the implementation of the Rehabilitation Scheme of sick MSMEs in the State.(*MSMEs Policy Note-2014-15; Government of Tamil Nadu. 2016 Pp.37*)

Chapter-XI

Thrust Areas for Corporate social Responsibility Programmes in MSMEs in India

11.1. Introduction

Corporate social Responsibility (CSR) is a concept whereby companies integrate social and environmental concerns in their business operations and in their interaction with their stakeholders on a voluntary basis. The Sustainability, Accountability and Transparency are three basic principles which together comprise all CSR activity.

The Sustainability implies that society must use no more of a resource than can be regenerated. This can be defined in terms of the carrying capacity of the ecosystem and described with input–output models of resource consumption. Viewing an organisation as part of a wider social and economic system implies that these effects must be taken into account, not just for the measurement of costs and value created in the present but also for the future of the business itself. Measures of sustainability would consider the rate at which resources are consumed by the organisation in relation to the rate at which resources can be regenerated.

The Accountability of an organization is concerned with recognizing that its actions affect the external environment, and therefore assuming responsibility for the effects of its actions. This concept implies recognition that the organisation is part of a wider societal network and has responsibilities to that entire network rather than just to the owners of the organisation.

Transparency, as a principle, means that the external impact of the actions of the organisation can be ascertained from that organization's reporting and relevant facts are not concealed within that reporting. So the Sustainability, Accountability and Transparency of an enterprise inspires necessarily its responsible management to prepare the CSR budget in every year to utilize the same towards the upgradation of wellbeing of the society where these companies are surviving and increase the standard of living of human beings.

In a nutshell, CSR is the Societal expectations of corporate behaviour; a behaviour that is alleged by a stakeholder to be expected by society or morally required and is therefore justifiably demanded of a business CSR is not always a legal necessity; increasingly it is an obligation. However a company has to be socially responsible even though it is not a legal obligation

11.2. Need of CSR Programmes in India

The India as a state has facing lot of problems with its developmental scenario .There are lot of social, Cultural, traditional issues in this society. At present, increased cost of private school education, lack of sufficient number of schools at remote areas, lack of proper and timely medical facilities in rural areas, increased of medical costs in urban areas, Conflict between the castes, untouchable or treating as a second hand persons of a particular community of people in very remote villages and discrimination by the name of caste and gender are major social issues.

The devaluation of Indian Cultural and Indian languages which has more than history of 4000 years, adoption of foreign culture which is not relevant to our society is disturbing the Indian corporate to interact with this issues.

In addition to it, reduced space for agricultural activities and increased usage of non organic inputs in agricultural activities, Industrial pollutions in all forms which is partially causing the Cancer, ulcer to the general public are major disadvantages of current industrial development. The modern industrial set up urges to its employees to work very hard for his survival. It results the stress, tension and occupational diseases.

The nature is also playing in the life of human being in the history of India. Heavy drought or over flood destroyed the agriculture which only one income source of majority of peoples in India. Tsumani, Cyclone, Flood, Drought are the important natural activities to disturbing peaceful living of the peoples of this state. Poverty and unemployment problem, under employment problems are the important challenges of current industrial development. It indicates the unequal distribution of nation income to its citizens of the state of India.

11.3. SSIs Units with CSR Budgets in India

The Majority of rural based SSIs Units are not ready to share its profit with its society. But now a day we can see the facelift of SSIs Units favourable manner towards the society development and social work. In this connection, Small scale Industrial estates   are started the CSR activities throughout the country. The tree plantations, Hospital services, primary school education and facilities for drinking water road maintenances work are some important CSR activities of our Indian small scale industrial estates. In addition to it, Youth development programmes and employees' skill development programmes are also implemented.

There is vast need to create the awareness and motivate the young and energetic small entrepreneurs in India to participate the following **Thrust Areas for Corporate social Responsibility Programmes.** In the state of Tamilnadu , Sakthi masala Group of Companies, Fire and printing industries of Sivakasi District, Locker industries of Dinidgul, TEA(Tiruppur Exports Associations), Coimbatore Textiles Industries and industries under cooperative fold such as Handloom, Fisheries, Cooperative Tea and Milk Industries are the important concerns in implementing the CSR programmes in Tamil Nadu. They are directly or jointly with other non government organisation executing the CSR programmes. In this connection, the following opt able programmes are discussed to be implemented under CSR activities in Tamilnadu State.

11.4. Thrust Areas for Corporate social Responsibility Programmes in India

11.4.1. Educational Services

1. Construction of class rooms/school buildings.
2. Renovation of existing primary school buildings.
3. Construction of sanitized toilets for girls of backward areas.
4. Providing furniture, electrical appliances, lab instruments to Govt. schools.
5. Supply of study materials like bags, books, stationery etc. to children belonging to the under privileged class of the society.
6. Scholarship or financial support to talented children of backward areas and Scholarships to meritorious students belonging to SC, ST, OBC and disabled categories.
7. Providing education and training for mentally and physically challenged children.
8. Adoption/construction of hostels especially for girls and SC&ST.

11.4.2. Electricity Facility

Providing electricity and solar lights to the areas in the vicinity of Project sites

11.4.3. Health and Family Welfare

1. Organizing health check-up camps, with particular focus on women, children, disabled and old age homes.
2. Contribution for construction of hospital buildings, dispensary, special wards.
3. Providing medical equipments to hospitals.
4. Providing mobile medical vans.

11.4.4. Irrigation Facilities

11.4.5 Sanitation and Public Health

11.4.6 Pollution Control

11.4.7 Animal Care

11.4.8. Promotion of Sports, Art and Culture

1. Providing sports equipments to the young and talented for promotion of sports.
2. Promotion of heritage by adoption and maintenance of historic monuments.

11.4.9. Employment and Training

1. Promotion of livelihood for economically weaker sections through forward and backward Linkages.
2. Setting up of skill development centers, Imparting Vocational Training, Skill training, entrepreneurship development and placement assistance programmes for youth and Entrepreneurship Development Programme(EDP).

11.4.10. Infrastructure and Rural Development

1. Construction of Community Centers/Night Shelters/Old Age Homes, Adoption/ Construction of Hostels (especially those for SC/ST and girls) and Building of Roads, Pathways and Bridges.
2. Adoption of villages.

11.4.11. Drinking Water Facility

1. Providing drinking water facility by installing tube wells /pumps/bore wells tanks/ ponds etc.
2. Setting up of pipe lines/extension of existing water pipelines.

11.4.12. Waste or Energy Management

1. Cleaner waste treatment processes.
2. Substitution of Hazardous chemicals with cleaner alternatives.
3. Responsible waste disposal practices.

11.4.13. Promotion of renewable Sources of Energy

11.4.14. Promotion Non-conventional Energy Sources

a. Energy efficiency
b. Energy conservation

11.4.15. *Biodiversity Conservation*

1. Land rehabilitation.
2. Soil conservation.
3. Rain-water harvesting and replenishing the ground water supply.
4. Aquifer recharging.
5. Desalination plant.
6. Effluent reduction and control.
7. Watershed development.

11.4.16. *Protection, Conservation and Restoration of Eco-system*

1. Reduction of carbon emissions through energy efficient and renewable energy technologies.
2. Promoting forestry programmes; Taking action on points suggested by Ministry of Forest.
3. Activities related to the preservation of the Environment & Ecology and to Sustainable Development.
4. Implementation of Environment friendly technologies in the production process.
5. Greening the supply chain, and innovation in products and services which have a clear and tangible impact on environmental sustainability fall under this category of activities.
   a. Green buildings.
   b. Reduction of air emission.
   c. Reduction of noise emission (Beyond Compliance).
   d. Green audit.

11.4.17. *Disaster Management*

1. Up to 5% of the annual budget for CSR and Sustainability activities has to be earmarked for Emergency needs, which would include relief work undertaken during natural calamities/disasters, and contributions towards Prime Minister's/Chief Minister's Relief Funds and/or to the National Disaster Management Authority. Such contributions would count as valid CSR and Sustainability activities.
2. Relief to victims of Natural Calamities like earthquake. Cyclone drought & flood situation in any part of the country.
3. Disaster Management Activities including those related to amelioration! Mitigation.

11.5. Conclusion

The business organizations of a particular society must consider not only better utilization of sources of that society but also provide more attention for that society development. In this connection, some percentage of funds must be allotted for its CSR programme. In addition to it, it should share the expenses of government and other NGOs CSR activities. India mainly consists of agricultural area where the lot of thrust for development in all aspect. So the major contribution of CSR programmes is for the protection of Agricultural Sector. It is an essential duties of Industrial organisation to introduce the Organic production facilities in this segment. In addition to it, the adequate measures and training progrmmes should be initiated for better performance of CSR. New thrust area like as orphanage, cultural development activities and poverty elimination programmes should be added. The awareness programme for CSR activities, performance appraisal system for CSR should be implemented.

References

1. Policy note on Department of Hand looms and textiles, Government of Tamilnadu, 2014-2015.

2. Recommendation and Conventions on Corporate Social Responsibility, UN Publications, USA, 2009.

3. Annual report of Micro, Small and Medium Enterprises, Government of India, 2014-15.

4. Reetu Sharma, "Problems and prospects of small scale industrial units (A case study of exporting and non-exporting units in Haryana)", Asia Pacific Journal of Marketing & Management Review, Vol.1, No. 2, October 2012.

5. Udyog Yug-July 2004.

6. B. Ravikkumar, "A Study on Human resource management Practices of Handloom Weavers Cooperative Societies in Dinidgul and Madurai Districts of Tamilnadu", Unpublished Thesis Gandhigrm Rural Institute Deemed University, Gandhigram, 2014-2015.

7. Policy Notes of Micro, small and Medium Enterprise, Government of Tamil Nadu, 2014-2015.

8. Financial Statement Analysis for Small Businesses-A Resource Guide, Virginia Small Business Development Centre Network, 2011.

9. K. Aswathapra, "Essential of Business Environment", Himalya Publishing House, Mumbai 2001.

10. S.N. Chary, "Production and operations management", Tata MC-Graw Hill publishing company Limited, New Delhi, 1988.

11. P.B Appa Rao, "Personnel problems in small scale industry", Deep and Deep, New Delhi, 1989.

12. Vasanth desai, "Management of small scale industries", Himalaya publishing house, New Delhi, 1990.

13. Drucker and F. Peter, "Innovation and Entrepreneurship", Heinemann: London, 1985.

14. M.C Gupta, "Entrepreneurship in small scale industry", An mol publications, New Delhi, 1987.

15. "Survey on Structure and Promotion of Small Scale Industries in India", Government of India NACAER & FNS, December, 1993.

16. Industrial policy Resolution, Government of India, 2005-06.

17. Ministry of Finance and Economic Division, Economic Survey, Government of India, 1999-2003.

18. K.V. Ramaswamy, "Small scale manufacturing industry: some aspect s of size, growth and structure", Economic and political weekly, Feb.1994.

19. T.A. Bhavani, "Small Scale Units in Era of Globalization: Problems and Prospects, Economic and Political Weekly", Vol. XXXVII, 2002.

20. C.L. Bansal, "Entrepreneurship and Small Business Management", Har-Anand Publications, Delhi, 1998.

21. Goyal and Alok, Business Environment, V.K Publisher, Delhi, 2004.

22. C.R. Kothari, "Research Methodology, Methods and Techniques", Wiley Eastern Limited, New Delhi, 2000.

ABBREVIATIONS

Abbreviation	Full Form
ARIW	Agro-Rural Industries wing
CCRI	Central Coir Research Institute
CFTI	Central Footwear Training Institute
CICT	Central Institute of Coir Technology
CGTMSE	Credit Guarantee Trust for Micro and Small Enterprises
CLCSS	Credit Linked Capital Subsidy Scheme
CSR	Corporate Social Responsibility
DC (MSME)	Development Commissioner (Micro, Small and Medium Enterprises)
EM	Entrepreneurs Memorandum
EDP	Entrepreneurship Development Programme
ESDP	Entrepreneurship-cum-Skill Development Programme
FTS	Field Testing Station
GoI	Government of India
ICT	Information and Communication Technology
IIE	Indian Institute of Entrepreneurship
IPR	Intellectual Property Rights
KVI	Khadi and Village Industries
MGIRI	Mahatma Gandhi Institute for Rural Industrialisation
M/o MSME	Ministry of Micro, Small and Medium Enterprises
MSE	Micro and Small Enterprises
MSE-CDP	Micro and Small Enterprises – Cluster Development Programme
MSME-DO	Micro, Small and Medium Enterprises –Development Organisation
MSME	Micro, Small and Medium Enterprises
MSMED Act	Micro, Small and Medium Enterprises Development Act

MSME-DI	Micro, Small and Medium Enterprises Development Institute
MSME-TC	Micro, Small and Medium Enterprises Testing Centre
MSME-TDC	Micro, Small and Medium Enterprises Technology Development Centre
MSME-TS	Micro, Small and Medium Enterprises Testing Station
MSME-TR	Micro, Small and Medium Enterprises Tool Room
MSME-TI	Micro, Small and Medium Enterprises Training Institute
NB MSME	National Board for Micro, Small and Medium Enterprises
NER	North-Eastern Region
NIESBUD	The National Institute for Entrepreneurship and Small Business Development
NIMSME	National Institute for Micro, Small and Medium Enterprises
NMCP	National Manufacturing Competitiveness Programme
NSIC	National Small Industries Corporation Limited
NTSC	NSIC Technical Service Centre
O/o DC MSME	Office of Development Commissioner(MSME)
PMEGP	Prime Minister's Employment Generation Programme
QMS	Quality Management System
QTT	Quality Technology Tools
R&D	Research & Development
REGP	Rural Employment Generation Programme
REMOT	Rejuvenation, Modernisation and Technology Upgradation of the Coir Industry
SDP	Skill Development Programme
SFURTI	Scheme of Fund for Regeneration of Traditional Industries
SME	Small & Medium Enterprises
SSI	Small Scale Industries
UN	United Nations